LEADING
INNOVATION
AND CHANGE

NASPA™
Student Affairs Administrators
in Higher Education

LEADING INNOVATION AND CHANGE

A Guide for Chief Student Affairs Officers on Shaping the Future

LAURENCE N. SMITH, ALBERT B. BLIXT,
SHANNON E. ELLIS, STEPHEN J. GILL, AND KEVIN KRUGER

◆ NASPA™
Student Affairs Administrators
in Higher Education

NASPA.
Student Affairs Administrators
in Higher Education

Leading Innovation and Change: A Guide for Chief Student Affairs Officers on Shaping the Future

Published by

NASPA–Student Affairs Administrators in Higher Education
111 K Street, NE
10th Floor
Washington, DC 20002
www.naspa.org

Additional copies may be purchased by contacting the NASPA publications department at 202-265-7500 or visiting http://bookstore.naspa.org.

NASPA does not discriminate on the basis of race, color, national origin, religion, sex, age, gender identity, gender expression, affectional or sexual orientation, or disability in any of its policies, programs, and services.

Library of Congress Cataloging-in-Publication Data

Smith, Laurence N.
  Leading innovation and change : a guide for chief student affairs officers on shaping the future / Laurence N. Smith, Albert B. Blixt, Shannon E. Ellis, Stephen J. Gill, and Kevin Kruger.
    pages cm
  Includes index.
  ISBN 978-0-931654-75-6
  1. College student personnel administrators--United States. 2. Student affairs services--United States. I. Title.
  LB2343.S549 2015
  378.1'12--dc23
                          2014037741

Printed and bound in the United States of America
FIRST EDITION

Dedicated to the memory of the late Ron Lippitt and Kathie Dannemiller, pioneering giants whose work on innovation and change informed and guided us as we wrote this book. They were colleagues, mentors, and friends. They helped make the world a better place.

Contents

The Authors

Laurence N. Smith is cofounder and senior partner of New Campus Dynamics, a consulting company that helps colleges and universities build their leadership, innovation, and change solutions and capacity to successfully survive and thrive in the future. Smith is emeritus vice president for university marketing and student affairs at Eastern Michigan University, founder and first chair of NASPA–Student Affairs Administrators in Higher Education's James E. Scott Academy for Leadership and Executive Effectiveness after being appointed by Jim Scott, then president of NASPA. He is also a recipient of NASPA's Fred Turner Award in recognition of his outstanding service to the association. His creative approaches to innovation and change management, organizational revitalization, and executive coaching, as well as his lecture series on "Understanding Changing America," keep him in high demand as a keynote speaker, workshop presenter, and consultant in both the public and private sectors.

Albert B. Blixt is cofounder and managing partner of New Campus Dynamics. Blixt is an expert on designing and implementing rapid strategic change in complex organizations and a developer of the Whole-Scale Change methodology. As a senior partner in the internationally recognized consulting firm of Dannemiller Tyson Associates, he has worked with Fortune 500 firms, state and federal agencies, nonprofit organizations, and secondary and higher education institutions.

Shannon E. Ellis has worked in higher education as a faculty member and administrator for more than 30 years. Ellis's interests lie at the intersection of transformational leadership, strategy, and technology. Since 1998 she has served as vice president for student services at the University of Nevada, Reno, where she has been successful in her visionary and skillful leadership approaches to innovation and change. Among her many contributions to the student affairs profession, she served as NASPA president from 2000 to 2001.

Stephen J. Gill is an organizational learning consultant in both the private and public sectors, and a blogger, book author, community college trustee, and former board president. Gill is a recognized expert in the field of training and performance management and has served as a faculty member in the colleges of education at both the University of Wisconsin–Milwaukee and the University of Michigan.

Kevin Kruger is president of NASPA and the profession's spokesperson and representative to international and national higher education professional associations, foundations, government agencies, and media. He is widely known for his leadership initiatives to enhance the association's role in public policy, research, professional development, and student learning and assessment, with a particular interest in the use of technology in serving diverse student populations. His strong focus on leadership to secure the future of higher education—especially the role of student affairs— has resulted in his being a prominent speaker and contributor to a wide variety of higher education initiatives and programs.

Introduction

Laurence N. Smith and Albert B. Blixt

This book is a call to action. Higher education is at a tipping point. The world of higher education is changing, yet too many colleges and universities act as if it isn't.

The forces of change are multidirectional and inescapable, especially if you are in a leadership position. An increasingly complex, digital, and diverse world is emerging. It is a world that is shaking the foundations, values, guiding principles, mores, and customs as well as the very existence of many institutions of higher learning. New subjects are being taught in new ways to new types of students. Funding is shrinking, and accountability is becoming relentless. New technologies have altered the workplace, and there are increased demands for change in how student affairs professionals prepare students for post-college success. In this new world, those who adapt to new realities will survive and thrive. Those institutions that endure may look very different from the ones we have known.

On a growing number of campuses, divisions of student affairs and their executives have become increasingly vulnerable during times of shrinking resources, zero-sum resource allocations, and the internal competition for resources. During the past several years many student affairs divisions have been eroded through budget cuts, restructuring, or reassignment to other units, often with a loss of direct access afforded by reporting straight to the president.

The danger is that student affairs divisions will continue this decline precisely when they are most needed to support transformational change on campus. The risk is that student affairs divisions will become increasingly vulnerable as their fragmentation and realignment are mistakenly seen as acceptable by leaders seeking to cut costs or reallocate resources to fund other initiatives. This would be ironic at a time when these institutions are struggling with the challenge of attracting, retaining, and graduating students who need what student affairs should be designed to offer.

For higher education, the student experience is at the core of institutional success. A key lesson from the business sector is that the most important focus must be on attracting and retaining customers with products and services that meet their needs. The next generation of students will have different needs and different expectations. They will come directly from high school or they will transfer from a community college. They will be adult learners interested in retooling their skills or students from countries outside of the United States. They will live on campus or commute from home. They will learn in traditional classrooms and in virtual or hybrid settings. Myriad factors will affect their success. Student affairs professionals have the deepest

> *On a growing number of campuses, divisions of student affairs and their executives have become increasingly vulnerable.*

understanding of and most robust connection to students. They are best positioned to influence students' decisions and persistence from their first days on campus to their graduation.

CSAOs must respond by embracing a new vision for student affairs.

CSAOs must respond by embracing a new vision for student affairs, focusing not only on what must be changed but also on how they must evolve as professionals to be effective in the new order. To succeed in this new world, CSAOs must become strong, assertive, and competent leaders of innovation and change. Unfortunately, this will take many outside of their comfort zones. Some will remain in denial; others will look for painless solutions that make only cosmetic adjustments. Only those who embrace the challenge will survive and prosper.

This book is about leading innovation and change. At its core is the concept that the CSAO is in the best institutional position for performing this role. That is because student affairs is ideally positioned to provide transitional leadership through innovation and change.

Among the most important of the many forces that position the CSAO in this role are the changing demographics and psychographics of the new digital generation of students, increasing internal competition for shrinking financial resources, student expectations for outstanding delivery of programs and services, and new technologies transforming the delivery of programs and services.

Interviews with campus presidents and provosts indicate that the greatest obstacle facing CSAOs' transformational leadership is themselves. Conversations with many CSAOs suggest their reluctance is not lack of desire but lack of ideas and information about how to proceed. For some, risk taking and fear of failure are the obstacles. For others, their inability to embrace a new mission and vision for student affairs is what limits leadership.

HOW TO READ THIS BOOK

As its title states, this book is a guide for chief student affairs officers. It offers a collection of ideas, projects, strategies, tactics, tools, and techniques that will help CSAOs—as well as other student affairs executives and aspirants—assert themselves as central to the success of their institutions and as core members of the leadership team. The themes in this book deal with transformational leadership in innovation and change. We are quick to point out that although the book is focused on CSAOs and other leaders in student affairs, it has equal relevance for other college and university leaders who wish to play a key role in transforming their institutions to survive and thrive in turbulent times.

Chapter 1, The Case for Change, examines how demands for higher education reform are affecting universities and colleges and impacting student affairs. It also explores how changing demographics affect student retention and how an evolving workplace requires a new approach to student preparation.

Chapter 2, The CSAO Leadership Role, discusses the nature of the challenge facing the CSAO's leadership role and of creating an innovative and change-oriented division of student affairs. It discusses the sources of leadership power, balancing leadership and management roles, and overcoming the traps that block success.

Chapter 3, The Innovative Mind, explores the concept of innovation and how it affects organizational systems. It explains disruptive and sustainable innovations, how innovations create value, and how innovations relate to outcomes.

Chapter 4, Making Student Affairs the Hub of Innovation, begins with the observation that the student affairs function is becoming increasingly vulnerable on some campuses at a time when it can become the most valuable asset for innovation. The chapter makes the case for how the CSAO can lead innovation and describes the steps for doing so.

Chapters 5 through 8 move beyond the innovation process to cover change and the implementation of new ideas. Chapter 5, The CSAO and the "Secret Formula for Change," describes the conditions that must be present for an organization to overcome resistance to change. Chapter 6, The CSAO as Visionary, investigates the need for a compelling vision at the heart of the strategic planning process. Chapters 7 and 8, The CSAO as Change Architect and The CSAO as Change Champion, respectively, provide a detailed approach for the leader to understand, design, guide, and achieve systemic transformational change. These chapters recognize that innovation and systemic transformation require different processes and skills. Innovators and change agents need different tools for achieving success. Often the innovation team and change team require separate members but need to collaborate and communicate for optimizing results.

Chapter 9, Technology and Transformation, builds on the concept that the disruptive nature of rapidly developing technologies drives the need for transformation. The chapter describes the impact of technology on the CSAO for piloting innovation and change and the new roles technology will play in the future success of student affairs. The chapter provides guiding principles that will help the CSAO navigate leading both innovation and change.

Chapter 10, Technology and Rethinking the Student Affairs Service Model, explores new rules for moving from a reactive to a proactive service model. It considers mastering new tools of student engagement and ideas for creating interactive methods for student service delivery. It stresses staying abreast of changes among students who increasingly are digital natives and notes the need for an adaptive new student affairs model to be a vital institutional force.

Chapter 11, Building Capacity for Innovation and Change—Creating a Learning Culture, examines the necessity for higher education institutions and specifically student affairs to develop a learning culture. The chapter defines what it means for student affairs to be a learning organization and how it can influence the student outside of the classroom experience and enrich the total academic journey. The chapter's insights will help the CSAO formulate a strategic approach for getting staff on board, focused, and effective.

Chapter 12, Mobilizing Student Affairs for Innovation, presents a detailed case study that illustrates how a vice president for student affairs developed a comprehensive plan for innovation and change to produce an outstanding total student experience. The chapter provides concrete examples for applying the strategies and tools provided in the preceding chapters to implement innovation and change.

Chapter 13, The Way Forward, concludes the book by noting that the ideas presented within this text provide perspectives and choices for CSAOs on how to respond to the opportunities that confront their institutions and divisions of student affairs. The chapter advises CSAOs on how to navigate change, deal with failure, and avoid pitfalls in order to secure a positive and sustainable future.

ACKNOWLEDGMENTS

We thank our collaborators in writing this book, as well as those on whose ideas we built our approaches to leadership, innovation, and change. To those who encouraged and embraced our efforts over the years, we owe special appreciation. We learned with them and from them as we helped their campuses and organizations confront forces of change with new initiatives and courageous leadership.

We also express our sincere appreciation to NASPA–Student Affairs Administrators in Higher Education for publishing this work and hope that it opens new pathways for improving and growing the student affairs practice and impact. Special thanks to Melissa Dahne for her editing and singular efforts in bringing this book to life.

CHAPTER 1

The Case for Change

Kevin Kruger

Harvard Business School Professor John P. Kotter (1995), widely recognized as one of the foremost experts on change, said this about leading change: "Guiding change may be the ultimate test of a leader—no business survives over the long term if it can't reinvent itself" (p. 2). Kotter articulated the need for leaders to understand change as a process, one that involves a series of steps necessary to achieve positive results. Efforts at change take on many names—and certainly, higher education has seen its share of these: total quality management, reengineering, rightsizing, restructuring, and cultural change, among others. These change efforts have served as placeholders for the process of organizational change. Kotter maintained that most organizations fail during the change process due to a failure or lack of leadership.

Kotter (2007) noted that "management's mandate is to minimize risk and to keep the current system operating. Change, by definition, requires a new system, which in turn always demands leadership" (p. 3). This statement reflects the main themes of this book: executive leadership and the compelling need to recognize the demand for major changes in higher education in general and in student affairs in particular. To that end, it is critical that today's student affairs leaders recognize the first and most important step in the change process: *Establishing a Sense of Urgency.*

THE PREDICTED DOOM OF HIGHER EDUCATION IS A DIRECT THREAT TO STUDENT AFFAIRS

Higher education has been the subject of "doom and gloom" predictions for some time. Noted organizational expert Peter Drucker, quoted in a 1997 *Forbes Magazine* article, famously heralded the end of higher education:

> The current setup is doomed, at least so far as higher education is concerned. "Thirty years from now the big university campuses will be relics. Universities won't survive. It's as large a change as when we first got the printed book.... Such totally uncontrollable expenditures, without any visible improvement in either the content or the quality of education, means that the system is rapidly becoming untenable. Higher education is in deep crisis." (Lenzer & Johnson, 1997, p. 1)

Although Drucker's dire predictions were issued more than 17 years ago, since then the popular media have taken up the cause;

few weeks go by without a scathing denunciation of higher education in the news. Critics on one side point to the rising cost of higher education, while others question its value. Headlines shout, "Is College Worth It?" on a weekly basis. A recent *Wall Street Journal* article, "Degrees of Value: Making College Pay Off," is representative of current media critiques of higher education. The article points to a compelling need for change:

> What's really needed in U.S. higher education is major structural change. To remain viable, colleges and universities need to cut expenditures dramatically. For decades, they have ridden the student loan gravy train, using the proceeds to build palatial buildings, reduce faculty teaching loads and, most notably, hire armies of administrators. (Reynolds, 2014, para. 11)

This same article, in a replay of Drucker's 1997 prediction, suggests that modern colleges and universities will no longer be viable, but that their facilities can be used as "hotels" for students who want a traditional college experience: "Don't bother hiring faculty: Just bring in your courses online, with engineering from Georgia Tech, arts and literature from Yale, business from Stanford and so on" (Reynolds, 2014, para. 23).

Few weeks go by without a scathing denunciation of higher education in the news.

The increase in critiques of higher education and the calls for reform have been amplified in the past 10 years as the public perception of tuition costs has reached a tipping point. Many of these articles describe the "country club" atmosphere of new buildings and facilities and an "arms race" in which competing institutions are compelled to build new state-of-the-art academic buildings, residence halls, and recreation facilities. Among critics, the "rock climbing wall" has become the symbol of the college excess that has led to skyrocketing tuition costs and student debt. The headlines really capture it best. "Resort Living Comes to Campus" (*Wall Street Journal*, 12/6/2012); "Are College Students Spoiled?" (*Psychology Today*, 9/18/2013); and "Why Are Colleges Getting So Expensive?" (*The Atlantic*, 12/4/2013) are examples of the hundreds of articles that have reinforced a basic position: College is too expensive and "country club" amenities and an administrative hiring boom are to blame.

This last point—the increase in hiring of student service administrators—has sparked increasing discussion and controversy. More important, this area has created a significant vulnerability for student affairs leaders. The 2014 Delta Cost Project report "Labor Intensive or Labor Expensive?" identified a number of cost drivers that have resulted in the "skyrocketing" tuition increases and trillion-dollar student debt. Of particular interest are two findings that will increase the public scrutiny of student affairs:

> **Growth in administrative jobs was widespread across higher education—but creating new professional positions, rather than executive and managerial positions is what drove the increase.** Professional positions . . . grew twice as fast as executive and managerial positions at public non-research institutions between 2000 and 2012 . . .

Colleges and universities have invested in professional jobs that provide noninstructional *student* services, not just business support. Across all educational sectors, wage and salary expenditures for student services (per FTE staff) were the fastest growing salary expense in many types of institutions between 2002 and 2012. (Desrochers & Kirshstein, 2014, p. 3)

Clearly, college cost issues will continue to be a major force in the reform movement in higher education. A key leadership challenge will be to continue to provide a high level of student support and student services in a very conservative fiscal environment. In addition, as public scrutiny of costs continues, it will be critical for student affairs leaders to have access to data that support institutional investment in key administrative positions.

This need for urgency and change is echoed throughout the literature of higher education. Michael Barber, Katelyn Donnelly, and Saad Rizvi (2013), in their thoughtful paper, "An Avalanche Is Coming: Higher Education and the Revolution Ahead," stated that a "radical and urgent transformation is required in higher education as much as it is in school systems" (p. 3). They expressed concern that due to complacency, caution, or anxiety, the pace of change will be too slow and the nature of change too incremental (Barber, Donnelly, & Rizvi, 2013).

Perhaps no single perspective has gotten more attention from within and outside of higher education as the notion of disruptive innovation.

Perhaps no single perspective has gotten more attention from within and outside of higher education as the notion of "disruptive innovation." This concept, developed by Clayton Christensen and Henry Eyring (2011) in their book *The Innovative University,*

> *The compelling need for change in the next decade will largely be due to a series of macro forces that have aligned to challenge higher education.*

makes the case that higher education has thrived in a world supported by prestige and loyalty from alumni and state legislators without the innovations that would threaten the basic model of higher education. In this environment, change has not been necessary. Christensen and Eyring (2011) go on to say that the environment has changed dramatically:

Costs have risen to unprecedented heights, and new competitors are emerging. A disruptive technology, online learning, is at work in higher education, allowing both for-profit and traditional not-for-profit institutions to rethink the entire traditional higher education model. Private universities without national recognition and large endowments are at great financial risk. So are public universities. (p. 18)

It is certainly up for debate as to whether a commercial-style disruption is coming to higher education. Higher education is not Blockbuster or Borders Books, which met their demise because they failed to adequately adapt to the digital age. However, there is no question that technology is disrupting the traditional classroom and the traditional college experience. Following a decade of continual growth, 32% of students now report taking at least one online course (Allen & Seaman, 2013). With almost 70% of academic leaders believing that online education will be critical to the long-term strategy of their institutions, the impact of online education will only increase (Allen & Seaman, 2013). Flipped courses, hybrid courses, massive open online courses (MOOCs), competency-based education, and other technology-enabled learning experiences are changing the academy. All of these will change the very nature of the college experience—for all students—but particularly for traditional first-time, full-time students. Chapters 9 and 10 in this book will explore the ways in which technological changes will challenge student affairs leaders in the next decade.

SHEER NUMBERS AND NEW DEMOGRAPHICS ARE KEY CHANGE DRIVERS

The compelling need for change in the next decade will largely be due to a series of macro forces that have aligned to challenge higher education in an historic manner. Among higher education leaders, it is widely said that this period of higher education—the second decade of the new millennium—is unlike any other. Providing campus leadership during this transformational time will be critical. It is this imperative that makes this book so timely.

A key issue facing higher education will be significant changes in the numbers and characteristics of students graduating from high school. The Western Interstate Commission for Higher Education's annual publication *Knocking at the College Door: Projections of High School Graduates* outlines the challenge of the next decade: the number of students who will graduate from American high schools will decrease. After a long period of growth, the number of high school graduates peaked in the 2011–2012 academic year. While there will be wide disparities in regional numbers, nationally, the number of high school graduates will decline or hold steady until 2024, when there will be a small period of expansion (Prescott & Bransberger, 2012). The net effect of these changes will vary significantly by state and region. During this same period, 20 states will experience slight to aggressive growth in the number of high school graduates, while 24 states will experience moderate to slight decreases in high school graduates (5% to 15%). Six states will experience a more than 15% decrease in high school graduates (Prescott & Bransberger, 2012). Regardless of the region or state, it is clear that demographics are going to have a significant effect on the fiscal pressure facing most institutions, while at the same time, the overall competition for students will increase. Student affairs leadership during this period will be increasingly important. Enrollment management strategies will need to be retooled, enrollment and academic talent projections will need to be adjusted, and the financial viability of residence halls, student unions, and food service and recreation facilities will need to be carefully examined. In particular, fee- and enrollment-based financing will be challenged.

As the number of high school graduates declines over the next decade, another seismic shift will occur. The racial and ethnic breakdown of high school students will change dramatically. By 2020, 45% of the nation's public high school graduates will be non-White compared with 38% in 2009 (Prescott & Bransberger, 2012). During this period, "the number of high school graduates of Hispanic

> *By 2020, 45% of the nation's public high school graduates will be non-White compared with 38% in 2009.*

descent is projected to increase noticeably in all states. Asian/Pacific Islander numbers will grow everywhere but in Wisconsin and Hawaii" (Prescott & Bransberger, 2012).

Nationally, the data suggest a major shift in the demographics of the United States. As reflected in Figure 1.1, the number of Hispanic high school graduates will increase by 41% by 2019–2020 and 68% by 2024–2025. Adding to the effect of birth rates on high school graduates will be the effect of immigration patterns in the United States:

> Though different regions are home to very different shares of foreign-born populations, immigrants to the U.S. are more likely to be found in the West than in other regions. . . . This trend is driven by immigrants born in Asia and Latin America, who make up considerably larger shares of the West's overall population than those of other regions. (Prescott & Bransberger, 2012, p. 33)

Overall, these forces will change the racial/ethnic climate on most college campuses. Campus climate, diversity, and inclusivity issues will become more paramount during the next decade as this demographic shift works its way through college admissions, providing another challenge for student affairs leaders.

Figure 1.1. *Cumulative Percent Projected Change in U.S. Public High School Graduates Relative to 2008–2009, by Race/Ethnicity*

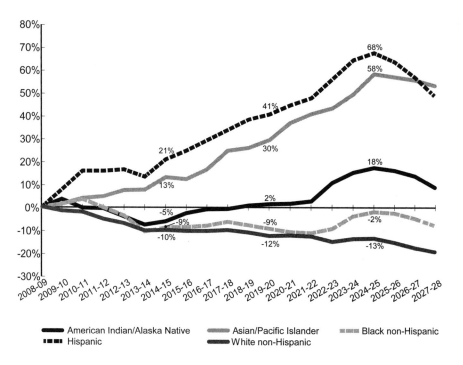

Note. Adapted from Prescott & Bransberger, 2012, p. 33. Reprinted with permission.

The challenge inherent in the increase in Hispanic and Native American students is that the college completion rate for these students is well below their White, non-Hispanic peers: "Unfortunately, it is a long-standing reality that educational success is very uneven. In particular, low-income and first-generation students, racial and ethnic minorities, immigrants and adults have traditionally been underrepresented among college students and graduates" (Lumina Foundation, 2013, p. 3). As illustrated in Figure 1.2, degree attainment by Hispanic adults is slightly more than 19% and Native American adults just under 24%.

Figure 1.2. *Degree-attainment Rates Among U.S. Adults (Ages 25–64), by Population Group*

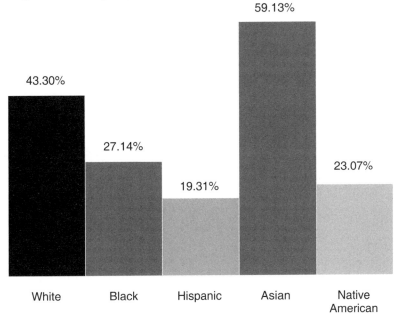

Note. Adapted from Lumina Foundation, 2013, p. 4. Reprinted with permission.

This harsh reality results in large cohorts of underrepresented Americans who cannot fully benefit from higher education and suffer significant economic consequences as a result. College attendance matters. A 2014 report by the Pew Research Center underscores this point: "On virtually every measure of economic well-being and career attainment—from personal earnings to job satisfaction to the share employed full time—young college graduates are outperforming their peers with less education" (p. 3). College graduates from the ages of 25 to 32 earn about $17,500 more annually than their peers with just a high school degree (Pew Research Center, 2014). In addition, the vast majority (86%) of these same college graduates see their job as a career or a stepping-stone to a career. Only 57% of high school graduates feel the same way (Pew Research Center, 2014).

WHAT WORKS IN STUDENT RETENTION IS CHANGING

Ensuring that students from underrepresented groups have access to college is a national imperative. However, the factors that affect college attainment and college completion for these students will be significantly different than for students up to now. The Hispanic students who will be graduating high school in the next decade are more likely to be first-generation college students than their White, non-Hispanic peers. "Demographically, first-generation students are more likely to be female, older, Black or Hispanic, have dependent children, and come from low-income families than students whose parents have college degrees" (Engle, 2007, p. 25). This new demographic of low-income, first-generation students will create a daunting challenge for higher education. Student affairs leadership will be vital in the

This new demographic of low-income, first-generation students will create a daunting challenge for higher education.

development of programs and support structures necessary for these students to attain a college degree.

Factors that have proven to be successful in retaining first-generation, low-income students provide an evidence-based foundation for student affairs to redirect resources. What has become clear is that the first-year experience is critical to the success of these students. The Pell Institute outlined the challenge we face:

> Low-income, first-generation students were nearly four times more likely—26 to 7 percent—to leave higher education after the first year than students who had neither of these risk factors. Six years later, nearly half (43 percent) of low-income, first-generation students had left college without earning their degrees. Among those who left, nearly two-thirds (60 percent) did so after the first year. (Tinto & Engel, 2008, p. 2)

Programs that front-load support during the freshman year and create engagement opportunities for these students have been found to be particularly effective. The same Pell Institute report suggested a set of effective practices that can increase the persistence and ultimate degree completion for first-generation, low-income students:

* **A structured freshman-year experience**. The programs often serve as the main point of entry for participants and as a "home base" to help students adjust to and integrate into the institution.
* **An emphasis on academic support**. Most services are focused on giving students the skills and confidence they need to achieve academic success.

✳ **An active and intrusive approach to advising.** These programs see their students more often than other programs. Programs also focus on the "whole student" in the advising process using a case management approach.

✳ **A plan to promote participation.** These programs place requirements on students to ensure they make use of and benefit from available services.

✳ **A strong presence on campus.** The most successful programs are part of larger service entities such as educational opportunity programs or learning centers rather than standalone programs. (Tinto & Engel, 2008, p. 27)

Subsequent research has uncovered similar themes, with an emphasis on creating intentional engagement opportunities for first-generation, low-income students. These students are more likely to attend part time, work full time or have substantial work responsibilities, live off campus, and participate less in cocurricular activities, athletics, and volunteer work (Strand, 2013). This results in an overall lack of engagement and puts these students at greater risk of low levels of degree progress. To this end, it is critical that institutions focus their attention on creating connections and community for these students. Successful practices involve a range of initiatives, including bringing students to campus early, focusing on support

> *It is critical that institutions focus their attention on creating connections and community for these students.*

services for academic achievement, helping prepare students for successful lives after college, using mentors, creating programs that build community and promote engagement, and involving family members in on-campus programming (Strand, 2013).

Historically, higher education was the primary driver of social mobility—but for most low-income students, this economic path is out of reach. When only 15% of students in the lowest socioeconomic quartile earn a bachelor's degree (compared with 61% in the top quartile), social mobility is out of reach for many Americans. As Andrew Kelley said so well, "Our system of postsecondary education does promote social mobility, but only for the small segment of low-income Americans who actually finish a credential" (Kelly, 2014, para. 6).

In order to meet the needs of a changing student demographic, student affairs leaders will need to make difficult decisions about the reallocation of resources. Given the economic climate in the United States, and the public concern over rising tuition rates, it is unlikely that new resources will be available to address the needs of these new students. It will be necessary to move staff and resources from existing programs to strengthen campus efforts to support first-generation, low-income students. This will be one of the greatest leadership challenges over the next decade.

A NEW APPROACH TO CAREER PREPARATION IS NEEDED IN THE NEW ECONOMY

As the cost of higher education at both public and private non-profit colleges and universities has risen over the past decade, so has the pressure to demonstrate that, in fact, a college degree matters. What was a foregone conclusion for decades is now being challenged. Perhaps college is not the fast track to economic success that it once was? One report surveyed a national sample of almost 5,000 college graduates and found that nearly half of them were unhappy with their careers and the extent to which their college had prepared them for a successful career. Even worse, 45% of those surveyed said they were in jobs that do not require a 4-year degree (McKinsey & Company, 2013). The Bureau of Labor Statistics reported that slightly less than half of college graduates are in jobs that require a college degree. The breakdown looks like this:

> *It will be necessary to move staff and resources from existing programs to strengthen campus efforts to support first-generation, low-income students.*

About 48 percent of employed U.S. college graduates are in jobs that the Bureau of Labor Statistics (BLS) suggests require less than a four-year college education. Eleven percent of employed college graduates are in occupations requiring more than a high-school diploma but less than a bachelor's, and 37 percent are in occupations requiring no more than a high-school diploma. (Vedder, Denhart, & Robe, 2013, p. 1)

Perhaps worse than the previous two reports were the economic data from the middle of the 2011 recession, when "about 1.5

million, or 53.6 percent, of bachelor's degree-holders under the age of 25 last year were jobless or underemployed, the highest share in at least 11 years" (Associated Press, 2012, para. 17).

The above data might suggest that the college degree has lost its value, but the statistics on salary and unemployment suggest a very strong premium for a college degree. As indicated earlier in this chapter, the Pew Research Center found that college graduates earned, on average, $17,500 more per year than high school graduates. The Pew Research Center also reported that in 2013, only 3.8% of 25- to 32-year-olds with a college degree were unemployed compared with 12.2% of those with a high school diploma (Pew Research Center, 2014). Other reports underscore this wage premium and the gradual change in the job market. This disparity was even greater during the great recession of 2009. It is simple—increasingly, employers in the United States are requiring a college degree for entry-level employment:

> *It is simple—increasingly, employers in the United States are requiring a college degree for entry-level employment.*

"The shift in the workforce from less-educated to more-educated has been a slow and steady process brought about by technological development and increased global competition that led to automation of the workplace and offshoring" (Carnavale, Jayasundera, & Cheah, 2012, p. 11). During this same period, the supply of workers who hold a bachelor's degree has increased, but not as fast as the demand for them. The result has been an ever-increasing wage premium for those who are in the workforce with a bachelor's degree (Carnavale, Jayasundera, & Cheah, 2012). In fact, over the past 25 years, the bachelor's wage premium has resulted in the average earnings of a bachelor's degree holder being "nearly twice as much as those of a worker with only a high school diploma" (Carnavale, Jayasundera, & Cheah, 2012, p. 12).

Perhaps as important as the bachelor's degree wage premium is the evolving consensus among employers about the skills and competencies required for success in today's modern, global workplace. This set of critical skills is part of the "value-add" that employers expect from college graduates. Given that the world of work is changing, these core competencies will be increasingly important. According to the Bureau of Labor Statistics and the Department of Labor, every year more than one third of the entire U.S. labor force changes jobs; today's students may have between 10 and 14 jobs by the time they are 38. Students entering the workforce this year will increasingly be in jobs that did not exist 10 years ago.

This rapidly changing world of work needs employees who have the analytical and entrepreneurial skills that will allow them to shift jobs multiple times in their careers.

This rapidly changing world of work needs employees who have the analytical and entrepreneurial skills that will allow them to shift jobs multiple times in their careers. Employers want students who have the initiative to lead (Chegg, 2013) and who can connect, learn from each other, and thrive in a world of rapid change (IBM, 2012).

Similar results were found in a survey of senior-level executives conducted by Hart Research Associates (2013) on behalf of the Association of American Colleges and Universities. Their research focused on the kinds of learning today's college students need to succeed in today's economy. The primary findings quantify an assumption that has always existed—the real value of the college experience comes not from just the transmission of knowledge in the classroom, but is a complex mix of learning opportunities that occur in rich, interactive class experiences combined with a range of engagement opportunities outside of the classroom. It is these engaged, active, and intentional experiences that have the greatest learning outcomes. As Kuh, Schuh, Kinzie, and Witt (2010) maintained, "What students *do* during college counts more for what they learn and whether they persist in college than who they are or even where they go to college" (p. 8). This simple statement is the foundation from which college students develop the skills and competencies necessary to compete in the modern economy.

> *Employers increasingly are in need of college graduates who can thrive in an innovative, complex work environment.*

These highly prized skills should become part of a new curriculum emphasized at all 2- and 4-year colleges. Employers increasingly are in need of college graduates who can thrive in an innovative, complex work environment: "Notably, employers indicate that they prioritize critical thinking, communication, and complex problem-solving skills over a job candidate's major field of study when making hiring decisions" (Hart Research Associates, 2013, p. 12). This same study found several other results that should serve as a roadmap for student affairs leadership. They point to a key set of skills and competencies that should be the focus of the cocurricular experience:

* Nearly all those surveyed (93%) agree, "a candidate's demonstrated capacity to think critically, communicate clearly, and solve complex problems is <u>more important</u> than their undergraduate major."

* More than nine in ten of those surveyed say it is important that those they hire demonstrate ethical judgment and integrity; intercultural skills; and the capacity for continued new learning.

* More than three in four employers say they want colleges to place *more emphasis* on helping students develop five key learning outcomes, including: critical thinking, complex problem-solving, written and oral communication, and applied knowledge in real-world settings. (Hart Research Associates, 2013, p. 1)

College matters

While the value of the college degree may have become somewhat tarnished during this last recession and the challenging employment market that has followed, there is still a huge individual and societal advantage to achieving a college degree. For the individual student, college pays off with a significant earnings premium and a significantly higher likelihood of employment. College degrees also are critical to the companies and organizations, both for-profit and nonprofit, that need talented college graduates in order to be successful. The development of the core skills identified above—critical thinking, complex problem-solving, intercultural communication, ethical decision making, and civic engagement—will require a realignment of resources to achieve the

> *What we need is a new approach to how we work with students in their journey to position them for success after graduation.*

results demanded by today's employers. Clearly, these data suggest that every college and university should take a close look at the functions and philosophy involved in career development and traditional career services. For many, the focus on the skills necessary for employment sounds too much like "vocationalism" (Curran Consulting Group, 2014). What we need is a new approach to how we work with students in their journey to develop career awareness and the experiences that will help position them for success after graduation. Fifty percent of those already in the workforce wish they had received more real-world experience while in college, and 30% wish they had started the career exploration process earlier. This reinforces the need to develop new strategies to engage students earlier and more actively in this process:

What we need is an integrated approach to helping students develop the skills, characteristics and knowledge that will

In some ways student affairs is facing a "perfect storm." The economic realities of higher education will mean that few new resources will be available.

change employers' minds about the potential of our students, and make graduates job ready on day one. This doesn't mean changing the nature of education; it just means being more intentional about connecting the dots for students between college and career. (Curran Consulting Group, 2014, para. 19)

This will require the kind of innovative and bold leadership discussed in later chapters of this book.

A New Leadership Challenge for Student Affairs

This chapter sets the stage for the critical challenge facing student affairs leaders in the next decade. A series of macro forces is changing the very core of the academic enterprise. In some ways student affairs is facing a "perfect storm." The economic realities of higher education will mean that few new resources will be available. Yet, the demands on student affairs to serve an increasingly complex set of issues continue to increase. We are serving a larger number of students who require psychological services; new cohorts of first-generation, low-income students will require academic and social support to succeed; more military veterans and active-duty armed service personnel are going to college; and increasing numbers of students will be hybrid learners taking a combination of campus-based and online courses and even more will be completing their entire degree online. All of these present a compelling leadership challenge for the chief student affairs officer and the division of student affairs.

REFERENCES

Allen, I. E., & Seaman, J. (2013). *Changing course: Ten years of tracking online education in the United States.* Retrieved from Babson Survey Research Group and Quahog Research Group website: http://www. onlinelearningsurvey.com/reports/changingcourse.pdf

Associated Press. (2012, April 23). Half of recent college grads underemployed or jobless. *Cleveland.com.* Retrieved from http://www. cleveland.com/business/index.ssf/2012/04/half_of_recent_college_ grads_u.html

Barber, M., Donnelly, K., & Rizvi, S. (2013). *An avalanche is coming: Higher education and the revolution ahead.* Retrieved from Institute for Public Policy Research website: http://www.ippr.org/assets/media/ images/media/files/publication/2013/04/avalanche-is-coming_ Mar2013_10432.pdf

Carnevale, A., Jayasundera, T., & Cheah, B. (2012). *The college advantage: Weathering the economic storm.* Washington, DC: Georgetown Public Policy Institute.

Chegg. (2013, Fall). *Bridge that gap: Analyzing the student skill index.* Retrieved from http://www.chegg.com/pulse

Christensen, C. M., & Eyring, H. J. (2011). *The innovative university: Changing the DNA of higher education from the inside out.* San Francisco, CA: Jossey-Bass.

Curran Consulting Group. (2014, February 9). *The big disconnect between college and career.* Retrieved from http://curranoncareers.com/big-disconnect-college-career

Desrochers, D. M., & Kirshstein, R. (2014, February). Labor intensive or labor expensive? *Issue Brief*. Retrieved from American Institutes for Research Delta Cost Project website: http://www.deltacostproject. org/sites/default/files/products/DeltaCostAIR_Staffing_ Brief_2_3_14.pdf

Engle, J. (2007). Postsecondary access and success for first-generation college students. *American Academic, 3*, 25–48.

Hart Research Associates. (2013). *It takes more than a major: Employer priorities for college learning and student success.* Retrieved from https://www.aacu.org/leap/documents/2013_EmployerSurvey.pdf

IBM. (2012). *Leading through connections: Insights from the IBM Global CEO Study.* Retrieved from http://public.dhe.ibm.com/common/ssi/ ecm/en/gbe03485gben/GBE03485GBEN.PDF

Kelly, A. P. (2014). *Does college really improve social mobility?* [Blog post]. Retrieved from http://www.brookings.edu/blogs/social-mobility-memos/posts/2014/02/11-college-improve-social-mobility

Kotter, J. P. (1995). Leading change: Why transformation efforts fail. *Harvard Business Review, 73*(2), 59–67.

Kuh, G. D., Schuh, J. H., Kinzie, J., & Whitt, L. (2010). *Student success in college: Creating conditions that matter.* San Francisco, CA: Jossey-Bass.

Lenzner, R., & Johnson, S. S. (1997, March 10). Seeing things as they really are. *Forbes*. Retrieved from http://www.forbes.com/ forbes/1997/0310/5905122a.html

Lumina Foundation. (2013). A *stronger nation through higher education.* Retrieved from http://www.luminafoundation.org/publications/A_ stronger_nation_through_higher_education-2013.pdf

McKinsey & Company. (2013). *Voice of the graduate.* Retrieved from http://mckinseyonsociety.com/downloads/reports/Education/ UXC001%20Voice%20of%20the%20Graduate%20v7.pdf

Pew Research Center. (2014, February 11). *The rising cost of not going to college.* Retrieved from http://www.pewsocialtrends.org/2014/02/11/ the-rising-cost-of-not-going-to-college

Prescott, B. T., & Bransberger, P. (2012). *Knocking at the college door: Projections of high school graduates* (8th ed.). Retrieved from Western Interstate Commission for Higher Education website: http://www.wiche.edu/info/publications/knocking-8th/knocking-8th.pdf

Reynolds, G. H. (2014, January 15). Degrees of value: Making college pay off. *The Wall Street Journal.* Retrieved from http://online.wsj.com/news/articles/SB100014240527023038707045792983026378020002#printMode

Strand, K. J. (2013). *Making sure they make it: Best practices for ensuring the academic success of first-generation college students.* Retrieved from The Council of Independent Colleges website: http://www.cic.edu/Programs-and-Services/Programs/Walmart-College-Success/Documents/CIC-Walmart-Final-Report.pdf

Tinto, V., & Engel, J. (2008). *Moving beyond access: College success for low-income, first-generation students.* Retrieved from The Pell Institute website: http://www.pellinstitute.org/downloads/publications-Moving_Beyond_Access_2008.pdf

Vedder, R., Denhart, C., & Robe J. (2013). *Why are recent college graduates underemployed? University enrollments and labor-market realities.* Retrieved from Center for College Affordability and Productivity website: http://centerforcollegeaffordability.org/uploads/Underemployed%20Report%202.pdf

CHAPTER 2

The CSAO Leadership Role

Laurence N. Smith and Albert B. Blixt

[Leaders] don't make plans; they don't solve problems; they don't even organize people. What leaders really do is prepare organizations for change and help them cope as they struggle through it. (Kotter, 2001, p. 85)

The topic of leadership has spawned an extensive array of books, articles, research studies, courses, conferences, and seminars—as well as novels and plays—over the years. Indeed, there is enough reading matter on the subject to fill a lifetime. This chapter presents a few relevant concepts drawn from that enormous body of information to provide a common context for discussing the nature of the leadership challenge facing the chief student affairs officer (CSAO). It explores the leadership role of the CSAO in creating an innovative and change-oriented organization. The recommended ideas will also work well for any executive seeking the best methods to successfully lead innovation and change at any level in their organization.

The CSAO position comes with authority, accountability, and control to carry out the responsibilities of the office. The CSAO is expected to lead at the institutional and divisional levels as well as at other organizational areas they oversee. Within this context, CSAOs have choices to make regarding how they allocate their leadership, management, and administrative energies. The choices they make will define the outcomes they achieve.

Formal and informal leadership roles have boundaries of various kinds. These boundaries are set by higher education systems, boards, institutional missions, policies, shared or participative governance traditions, agreements, and collective bargaining contracts. There are also very real limits created by the hierarchy of reporting positions. However, no leadership boundaries are harder to break through than those leaders impose on themselves—internal boundaries that shape their personal perceptions, preferences, and behaviors in how they perform their roles. Often these boundaries are unconscious and therefore invisible. Making those limitations visible in order to deal with them is perhaps the most fundamental task a leader can undertake.

THE SOURCES OF LEADERSHIP POWER

There is no getting around it; the core of the CSAO's responsibility is the wise and effective use of power. Successful CSAOs know that how well they use their sources of power will determine what they achieve and the fate of the people under their administrative purview as well as the institution as a whole. The power to lead emanates essentially from nine sources under the CSAO's control.

> *There is no getting around it; the core of the CSAO's responsibility is the wise and effective use of power.*

1. **The power of position.** The CSAO is the boss, the chief, the head honcho. The CSAO position carries with it the power to establish organizational priorities, roles, and structures; the power to hire and fire; the power to allocate human and fiscal resources; the power to order actions to be taken; and the power to set (or at least influence) policy development and enactment. The power of the institutional position should not be arbitrary or permit capriciousness. But it is real, and provides the basis for strong leadership.

2. **The power of relationship.** The CSAO owns the platform for building trusting relationships with peers, superiors, and others not under his or her administrative control, as well as the ability to form teams, coalitions, and partnerships that span divisional or institutional boundaries.

3. **The power of information and insight.** Being central to institutional decision makers and the decision-making process, the CSAO is provided with opportunities to

gather and apply information. Possessing information that others do not have is a source of power. It can be used to guide one's own decisions as well as influence the decisions of others. Information, when used properly, helps the CSAO see things others do not see. This insight allows the leader to take wise action.

4. **The power to champion new ideas, innovations, and change.** The CSAO's leadership authority allows for creating, adopting, or adapting new approaches, programs, and services to better respond to the needs of students and other constituents.

5. **The power to leverage technology.** Technology is perhaps the most powerful driver of change in our society today. Technology makes it possible to manage information, make decisions, and communicate in ways not previously possible. Technology can release key personnel from having to participate in transactional activities so that the CSAO can direct human resources toward more value-added initiatives that focus on student well-being and institutional priorities.

6. **The power to shift the workplace culture.** Culture can be defined simply as "the way we do things around here." Culture consists of the set of assumptions, beliefs, attitudes, and values that guide behavior in any social system. Culture is often the factor that determines whether new ideas are generated and whether change initiatives succeed or fail. Chapter 11 is devoted to creating a culture of

organizational learning. The CSAO can build the support necessary for successful implementation of strategic change by both leading and participating in organizational learning related to innovation and change. Workplace culture seems to be ephemeral but it can be changed through highly visible leadership that shifts behaviors and attitudes.

> *Culture is often the factor that determines whether new ideas are generated and whether change initiatives succeed or fail.*

7. **The power of directing individual and organizational focus.** Leading innovation and change requires learned skills that CSAOs must possess to optimize their effectiveness in bringing about any desired organizational change. The ability to focus employees on desired outcomes, and supporting these efforts with recognition and reward when objectives are achieved, is an important CSAO resource that leads to new levels of productivity. Focus is directly related to having a compelling vision.

8. **The power of a compelling vision.** The ancient biblical saying, "Where there is no vision, the people perish" (Proverbs 29:18 King James Version) remains true today. A compelling vision that inspires, motivates, focuses, and empowers employees to achieve new levels of attainment is the stimulus for enthusiastic participation in innovation and change initiatives. Chapter 6, on the CSAO as

visionary, describes the importance of having a vision and engaging people to share it to bring about change.

Finally, perhaps the most important source:

9. **The power of personal belief, resolve, and resilience.** All CSAOs need to show their support of divisional and broader institutional visions by demonstrating their commitment to achieving them with the necessary passion, energy, resources, and time. In short, lead by example.

BALANCING LEADERSHIP AND MANAGEMENT ROLES: SIX TRAPS TO AVOID

Because all CSAOs have responsibilities as both leaders and managers, they are required to decide which role will dominate at any given moment. Complicating the decision is that CSAOs are team members as well as team leaders. As a member of the president's team, the CSAO must respond to the board and president's vision for the institution. However, CSAOs must also recognize that, regardless of whether they are acting at an institutional or divisional level, they are leaders invested with the responsibility and the latitude to lead by inspiring pursuit of both the institution's and division's visions for the future.

A compelling vision is the stimulus for enthusiastic participation in innovation and change initiatives.

The roles of manager (transforming resources into results) and administrator (maintaining transactional momentum) are both essential for organizational health. Allowing those roles to displace the leadership function is a real danger with several traps that wait for the unprepared leader.

Trap #1: Reverting to familiar behaviors. The first trap for CSAOs, especially those who have been appointed based on their success as managers or administrators, without prior real leadership experience, is to revert to these familiar roles rather than delegating them. Regretfully, given the choice between leadership and management activities, attention to management tasks often wins out. Sometimes it is a justifiable decision. But when a CSAO is seen as a manager instead of a leader, it invites many opportunities for eroding the long-term effectiveness of the CSAO and the division of student affairs.

Leadership guru Warren Bennis (1989) provided a comparison between leaders and managers that is useful in understanding the extremes of each function:

* Managers administer. Leaders innovate.
* Managers focus on systems and structure. Leaders focus on people.
* Managers rely on control. Leaders inspire trust.
* Managers have a short-range view. Leaders have a long-range perspective.
* Managers ask how and when. Leaders ask what and why.
* Managers' eyes are on the bottom line. Leaders look to the horizon.
* Managers imitate. Leaders originate.

* Managers accept the status quo. Leaders challenge it.

* Managers are classic good soldiers. Leaders are their own people.

* Managers do things right. Leaders do the right things. (p. 85)

Trap #2: Choosing personal preferences over organizational objectives. The leadership role is further complicated by the choice executives have to make between actively supporting the mission of the institution and division (organizational objectives [OOs]), or doing what they personally find more interesting, advantageous, and enjoyable, or less stressful and less threatening (personal preferences [PPs]). It is within this warring context that CSAOs must evaluate their priorities and performance. Difficult leadership initiatives (OOs) can be postponed easily under the guise of management activities—the putting out of daily fires and any number of other equally convenient excuses. A great stumbling block for success is that it is very easy to hide behind PPs, which can be justified or camouflaged to look like OOs.

> *When a CSAO is seen as a manager instead of a leader, it invites many opportunities for eroding the long-term effectiveness of the CSAO.*

Leading change is difficult. But it cannot be seen as an add-on to the responsibilities of the CSAO. It is at the core of the CSAO's role and, like accountability, cannot be delegated. Management tasks, however, can.

Trap #3: Failure to learn new skills and adopt a new mindset. Followers want and need their leader to lead. It is confusing to subordinates when CSAOs do not play a strong leadership role. The danger is greatest when managers, who previously have not played prominent leadership roles, are promoted to a CSAO position based on their successful management abilities and do not recognize that their promotion requires learning new leadership skills and developing a new mindset.

It is confusing to subordinates when CSAOs do not play a strong leadership role.

The new CSAO must develop a new skill set. Brian Tracy and Peter Chee (2013) asserted that leaders are made, not born. They define how they can achieve sustainable high performance for getting "extraordinary performance from ordinary people" (p. 3). Their list of disciplines for creating leadership excellence offers a good starting point for skills the CSAO must acquire. These include having a sense of mission, setting the example, demonstrating courage and integrity, being able to communicate, being able to inspire, being able to motivate others, being able to develop consensus, caring about people, and having focus, along with a strong commitment to continuous personal improvement, learning, and winning (Tracy & Chee, 2013).

The new CSAO must also adopt a new mindset required for his or her leadership role. The process for moving from management to leadership has been described as seven seismic shifts of perspective and responsibility (Watkins, 2012). Each of these shifts requires learning new skills and adopting the leader's mindset. Examples of the shift in roles from manager to leader include: "specialist to generalist, analyst to integrator, tactician to strategist, bricklayer to architect, problem solver to agenda setter, warrior to diplomat, and supporting cast member to lead role" (Watkins, 2012, pp. 66–67).

"Management is about coping with complexity" whereas "leadership by contrast is about coping with change."

John Kotter (2001) stated, "Leadership and management are two distinctive and complementary systems of action," (p. 85) noting that "management is about coping with complexity" (p. 86) whereas "leadership by contrast is about coping with change" (p. 86). He cautioned, "Strong leadership with weak management is not better, and is sometimes actually worse, than the reverse. The real challenge is to combine strong leadership and strong management and use each to balance the other" (p. 86).

Trap #4: Failure to acquire and practice emotional intelligence. No work on leadership can ignore the influence that Daniel Goleman has had with his groundbreaking research in the 1990s on emotional intelligence (EQ). The EQ components for success he identified include self-awareness, self-regulation, motivation, empathy, and social skill. Goleman found that successful leaders have high EQs, enabling them to manage and conduct themselves constructively with others. The bottom line is that "a person can have the best training in the world, an incisive, analytical mind, and an endless supply of smart ideas, but . . . still won't make a great leader [without having a high level of emotional intelligence]" (Goleman, 2004, p. 82).

Goleman's recent neuroscience research findings, reported in his 2013 book *Focus: The Hidden Driver of Excellence,* conclude that the primary task of leaders is to direct their own and their organization's attention. They can do so focusing on themselves to create self-awareness and self-control. They must also focus on others to understand their perspectives and to develop emotional empathy by feeling what someone else feels. Leaders also need to focus on the wider world to enhance their ability to devise strategy, innovate, and manage their organizations.

> *The primary task of leaders is to direct their own and their organization's attention.*

In other words, both formal and informal leaders can emerge if they can be comfortable in their own shoes and put themselves in the shoes of others. If, as they move up in the organization, they can maintain contact with former colleagues and friends, and if they can maintain their focus and assert themselves, sooner or later they will arrive at their destination.

Trap #5: Failure to have more than one leadership style. Paul Hersey and Kenneth H. Blanchard (1982) defined leadership as "any time one attempts to influence the behavior of an individual or group, regardless of the reason" (p. 3). They also differentiated leadership from management, stating that while leaders focus more broadly on an organization's mission and vision, management focuses on working with individuals and groups to accomplish organizational goals (Hersey & Blanchard, 1982).

Hersey and Blanchard (1982) are advocates of situational leadership, based on their findings that there is no single style of leadership appropriate for all settings. They noted that "effective leaders are able to adapt their style of leader behavior to the needs of the followers and the situation" (p. 94). They reported that when a leader's style is appropriate to a given situation, it is effective. When it is not appropriate, it is ineffective. This important distinction implies that "the difference between effective and ineffective styles is not the actual behavior of the leader but the appropriateness of this behavior to the environment in which it is used" (Hersey & Blanchard, 1982, p. 97). Of equal importance is their observation that "if the follower decides not to follow, it really doesn't matter what the boss thinks, what the nature of the work is, how much time is involved, or what the other situational variables are" (Hersey & Blanchard, 1982, p. 146).

Because no single leadership style is successful in all situations, successful leaders must be flexible in their approach. Although it is true that we want leaders to be authentic in their interactions with others, mastering more than one approach allows the leader to adapt to circumstances.

Goleman, Boyatzis, and McKee (2013) posited six different leadership styles that can be used to address specific situations:

* ***Visionary leadership: Moves people toward shared dreams.*** "Visionary leaders articulate where the group is going—but not how it will get there—setting people free to innovate, experiment, and take calculated risks. Knowing the big picture and how a given job fits in gives people clarity; they understand what is expected of them." (p. 57)

* ***Coaching leadership: Connects what a person wants with the organization's goal.*** "Coaches help people identify their unique strengths and weaknesses, tying those to their personal career aspirations. They encourage employees to establish long-term development goals.... Coaches are also good at delegating assignments that stretch them, rather than tasks that simply get the job done." (pp. 60–61)

* ***Affiliative leadership: Creates harmony by connecting people to each other.*** "The affiliative style represents the collaborative competence in action. Such leaders are most concerned with promoting harmony and fostering friendly interactions, nurturing personal relationships that expand the connective tissue with the people they lead" (pp. 64–65). Leaders need to beware of the danger of valuing feelings over performance. This style should not be used alone but in combination with the visionary or coaching style.

> *Mastering more than one approach allows the leader to adapt to circumstances.*

✴ *Democratic leadership: Values people's input and gets commitment through participation.* "[The] democratic approach works best when . . . the leader is uncertain about what direction to take and needs ideas from able employees. . . . Even if the leader has a strong vision, the democratic style works well to surface ideas about how to implement that vision or to generate fresh ideas for executing it. . . . However the democratic style can be counterproductive when it prolongs making crucial decisions, when employees are uninformed or incompetent." (pp. 67–68)

✴ *Pacesetting leadership: Meets challenging and exciting goals.* Pacesetting means the leader is able to outperform subordinates and uses that competence to drive others to improve. In doing so, "pacesetting leaders strive to learn new approaches that will raise their own performance and that of others" (p. 75). While pacesetting has its place, when it is applied poorly or excessively, or in the wrong setting, it can leave employees feeling pushed too hard and result in their becoming uninspired and unmotivated.

✴ *Commanding leadership: Soothing fears by giving clear direction in an emergency.* The "do it because I say so" style, when it works, does so when there is an urgency for action that demands immediate compliance with orders, usually given without explanation. However, in most situations it is the least effective and mostly counterproductive one. The short-term gains it creates are soon diminished by long-term turndowns resulting from low employee morale, resentment, and defection of top performers.

Although one of these leadership styles usually becomes dominant or most familiar and comfortable, different situations may require realigning the styles used to be most effective. Therefore, being facile with multiple leadership styles provides the leader with a wider array of options when they are needed. CSAOs who build their leadership team with members who have diverse leadership styles also have an obvious advantage—but only if they are willing to take the time to analyze what course of action will work best, and to acknowledge the complexities of leader–follower organizational relationships. Underscoring all leadership styles, successful outcomes depend on the emotional intelligence level of the leader and the leadership team.

Trap #6: Becoming isolated and losing touch: "It's lonely at the top" is a common lament of leadership. Among the most difficult tasks is truly knowing what the people in the

Few leaders realize how susceptible they are to their followers' influence.

organization think and how that thinking affects their behavior. It is hardly surprising to find countless stories about leaders mingling with their subordinates incognito, like Henry V the night before the battle of Agincourt, disguising himself to move about his army to learn firsthand what his soldiers truly thought of their chances.

Lynn Offermann (2004), professor of organizational sciences, reported that "few leaders realize how susceptible they are to their followers' influence." (p. 55). This is especially true when they rely on a very small group of colleagues who filter information to them. It is not uncommon for university and college executives to meet with representatives of constituent groups who have been selected by well-meaning but misguided staff to convey a rehearsed picture of what is supposed to be the sentiment of the campus. Offermann (2004) recommended that leaders need "a good set of values, some trusted friends, and a little paranoia to prevent them from being led astray" (p. 55). She stated that "most people—including leaders— prefer conformity to controversy," can be "fooled by flattery," start to believe their press, and "feel more entitled to privileges than others" (pp. 55–57). She proposed six ways to prevent this from happening:

1. Keep vision and values front and center.
2. Make sure people disagree.
3. Cultivate truth tellers.
4. Do as you would have done to you.
5. Honor your intuition.
6. Delegate don't desert, which means you have to "trust but verify." (p. 59)

Offermann (2004) advised leaders to behave as good examples doing what they are trying to accomplish, avoid group-think, refuse to fall prey to manipulative forces, associate with people who are fresh thinkers, allow honesty to take precedence over politeness, and to make sure that those who are not part of the team are called-out. She warned leaders to be suspicious of flattery, quoting cartoonist Hank Ketchum's remark that "flattery is like chewing gum.

Enjoy it, but don't swallow it" (Offermann, 2004, p. 59). She recommended to leaders that "one simple test of whether you're getting the feedback you need is to count how many employees challenge you at your next staff meeting" (Offermann, 2004, p. 60).

Offermann (2004) cautioned leaders to avoid being "cognitive misers' preferring the shortcuts of automatic thinking over considered examination," (p. 56) especially in situations where ideas are presented with considerable enthusiasm and there is a drive to come to quick acceptance without thinking about unintended consequences. She also warned about responding to the power of the majority or fears of undermining employee commitment by rejecting their recommendations, and suggested that each situation has to be evaluated against longer-term gains. Offermann (2004) noted the quote from former First Lady Rosalynn Carter, "A leader takes people where they want to go. A great leader takes people where they don't necessarily want to go but ought to be," and added that "in going against the tide, a leader will sometimes boost rather than undermine his or her credibility" (p. 57).

TWELVE LEADERSHIP ABSOLUTES

In his book *Lead*, Gary Burnison (2013), CEO of Korn/Ferry International, noted that "leadership can be learned and absorbed only by doing, starting with the most important lesson of all: to lead others, you must first lead yourself" (p. 4). Burnison (2013) organized leadership into 12 "absolutes," which provide closure to this chapter's exploration of the principles of leadership, innovation, and change. These absolutes can be a template for developing and measuring the CSAO's progress as a leader.

1. **Lead**, the first absolute, includes "grace and restraint," balancing "heroics with humility," recognizing that "words motivate, actions inspire," and always to take the "high road—always with no exceptions" (pp. 10–13).

2. **Purpose** is "the anchor of the organization" which must be overarching and "omnipresent—on the walls and in the halls" (pp. 28–29). It must be seen as the bridge to what the organization will be in the future, from what it is in the present.

3. **Strategy** is "not just direction, it's velocity," and velocity requires leadership to "shift the culture to match the execution timeline; "90 percent of strategy is execution and 90 percent of execution is people" (pp. 44–45). Strategy requires helping people understand the how so that they all go in the same direction, and letting them fill in the how by relying on their competence.

4. **People** need to be selected for leadership who possess the talent to lead, and leaders need to make sure that the right people are selected; their teams also have to be the right teams to accomplish things. "Finding the right players for your team and quickly letting go of those you come to realize are wrong for the job is the operational dimension of talent management" (p. 63).

5. **Measure and monitor** permits the leader "to avoid becoming the leader of the inevitable"; data are only as

useful as the leader's ability to filter and interpret them in context. The best advice is to "open your ears to what you don't want to hear; create a culture that does the same" (pp. 78–81).

6. **Inspire and empower** requires the leader to "relinquish some control" (p. 97) and to "make both failures and victories empowering milestones to success" (p. 99).

7. **Reward and celebrate** are summed up with advice to "win hearts and minds, not by pocketbooks," but by recognizing that "the best rewards enhance autonomy, mastery, and purpose" (pp. 110–111).

8. **Anticipate** requires being a good observer, being aware, and staying focused on what can be done now and not on what has always been done. It requires the leader to "always have a Plan B—and a backup for the backup" (p. 129).

> *90 percent of strategy is execution and 90 percent of execution is people.*

9. **Navigate** "is the process of translating Strategy and Anticipation in action. It is real-time, purposeful decision making, requiring you to be agile in the moment, yet always focused on the horizon" (p. 140). It is important to note that "inaction can be more dangerous than action, and failure to act is a choice" (p. 145).

10. **Communicate**, communicate, and communicate. "A leader is a change-maker, not a Roman Senator. You're looking to move people to action. That means your communication

needs to be interactive, creating true connection and stir-ring emotional response" (p. 156).

11. **Listen,** and by doing so recognize that "the distance between hearing and listening is thinking and under-standing" (p. 170).

12. **Learn**: "Knowledge breeds confidence; failure leads to wisdom" (p. 188). Furthermore, "continued success requires growth and growth requires learning" (p. 189). Leaders know what they don't know; successful leaders learn what they don't know from others and from trying out new ideas and solutions. As Thomas Edison said: "I have not failed 10,000 times. I have successfully found 10,000 ways that will not work" (p. 190).

Perhaps only a self-employed genius who has great success resulting in great wealth can afford to fail 10,000 times and cre-atively spin it as learning through experience. Interestingly, higher education has collectively had thousands of experiences that teach us what does not work. It is time to recognize that those who look only to the past for direction and try to ward off the forces of innovation and change will fail, not only repeating the past but also missing the opportunities inherent in the promise of the future.

Developing and applying these leadership qualities provides a pathway for CSAOs to assert themselves as successful key campus leaders, pioneers able to respond creatively to the significant chal-lenges and opportunities confronting higher education and lead the innovation and change initiatives that will help it remain viable as an outstanding national and global resource.

THE CSAO ROLE FOR LEADING INNOVATION

Knowing how to lead innovation is the key to establishing and sustaining a thriving organization in the 21st century. The concept that embodied the definition of leadership as having a vision and inspiring others to buy into it is increasingly becoming obsolete—unless, of course, the vision is to create an innovative organization.

Leading an innovative organization demands the emotional intelligence and wide array of skills set forth in this chapter. It also requires that the leader recognize and deeply hold to the concept that leading an innovation-focused organization is the pathway to the future and to survival.

Hill, Brandeau, Truelove, and Lineback (2014) reported that the leader's role in innovation is "not to come up with a vision and make innovation happen themselves" but to "create a place—a contact, an environment—where people are willing and able to do the hard work that innovative problem solving requires" (p. 3). They do this by creating organizations willing and able to innovate. The common elements that describe how leaders make sure their organizations are able to innovate include collaboration, engagement discovery-driven learning, and making integrative decisions (Hill, Brandeau, Truelove, & Lineback, 2014).

Leaders face a fundamental paradox in creating an innovative organization: They "need to *unleash* the talents of individuals *and*, in the end, to *harness* those talents in the form of a collective innovation that is useful to the organization" (Hill, Brandeau, Truelove, & Lineback, 2014, p. 26). What is most interesting about this idea is that many CSAOs have been doing this as an integral part of their leadership style. In other words, this should come naturally to CSAOs. What doesn't come naturally is that CSAOs do not necessarily feel empowered to do this on the institutional stage and are not familiar with how to use this skill set to create an innovative organization that leads the way for their institution.

As Hill, Brandeau, Truelove, and Lineback (2014) noted, collaboration also takes on a new context in creating an innovation-focused organization. Collaboration for innovation doesn't mean that everyone supports each other's ideas and that conflict is bad. Out of the heat of conflict often come the best ideas and innovations. Having and sharing differences is the melting pot for solutions. Good leaders need to create the environment that allows for conflict of ideas separate from the conflict of people who feel attacked for advancing a new idea or different approach (Hill, Brandeau, Truelove, & Lineback, 2014).

Hill, Brandeau, Truelove, and Lineback (2014) pointed out that creating discovery-driven learning also implies a paradox. It requires letting go of the goal setting, creating metrics, planning steps, striving to achieve end-results, and assigning responsibilities for making certain outcomes are focused on and attained (Hill, Brandeau, Truelove, & Lineback, 2014). The paradox is that this approach defines the outcomes and steps to achieve them before knowing what possibilities and new solutions innovation can create that go beyond recombining old, and often outmoded, ideas and practices (Hill, Brandeau, Truelove, & Lineback, 2014). Obviously, innovation is not a neat, easy process. As Hill, Brandeau, Truelove, and Lineback (2014) noted, other paradoxes of leading innovation include: fostering experimentation, learning, and performance; promoting improvisation and structure; showing patience and urgency; and encouraging bottom-up initiative and intervening top down.

Leading innovation requires rethinking the role of leadership, learning new approaches and how to deal with the paradoxes inherent in the leading innovation process, and having strong belief that the pathway to creating an innovation-focused organization will pay off with new levels of great ideas and energy to implement them.

REFERENCES

Bennis, W. (1989). *On becoming a leader.* Reading, MA: Addison-Wesley.

Burnison, G. (2013). *Lead.* Hoboken, NJ: John Wiley.

Goleman, D. (2004, January). What makes a great leader. *Harvard Business Review*, pp. 82–91.

Goleman, D. (2013). *Focus: The hidden driver of excellence.* New York, NY: HarperCollins.

Goleman, D., Boyatzis, R., & McKee, A. (2013). *Primal leadership: Learning to lead with emotional intelligence.* Boston, MA: Harvard Business Review Press.

Hersey, P., & Blanchard, K. (1982). *Management of organizational behavior: Utilizing human resource.* Englewood, NJ: Prentice-Hall.

Hill, L. A., Brandeau, G. T., Truelove, E., & Lineback, K. (2014). *Collective genius: The art and practice of leading innovation.* Boston, MA: Harvard Business Review Press.

Kotter, J. P. (2001, December). What leaders really do. *Harvard Business Review*, pp. 85–96.

Offermann, L. R. (2004, January). When followers become toxic. *Harvard Business Review*, pp. 55–65.

Tracy, B., & Chee, P. (2013). *12 disciplines of leadership excellence.* New York, NY: McGraw Hill Education.

Watkins, M. (2012, June). How managers become leaders. *Harvard Business Review*, pp. 64–72.

CHAPTER 3

The Innovative Mind

Laurence N. Smith and Albert B. Blixt

This chapter explores the concept of innovation and how it affects organizational systems. We will examine how chief student affairs officers (CSAOs) can make their divisions of student affairs the center of innovation on campus.

The terms "innovation" and "innovative" are tossed around so casually that their meanings have become obscured. Not all things that are touted as new are innovations. Often the term is used as a way to repackage and sell an existing product, service, or theory. *True* innovations are novel ideas for meeting needs or solving problems that are then given utility through implementation. Innovations result from the practical application of creative ideas. This often happens by connecting disparate notions, concepts, or inventions together to create the Idea, which then provides commercial value when connected to consumers.

51

DISRUPTIVE VS. SUSTAINING INNOVATION

Ideas change the world in two ways: either by improving the status quo or by disrupting it. *Sustaining innovations* are those that improve existing products, systems, or educational practices by making things bigger and better (Christensen & Eyring, 2011). Gasoline-powered automobiles are much, much better than those of a hundred years ago.

> *Ideas change the world in two ways: either by improving the status quo or by disrupting it.*

Today's cars have sophisticated electronics, power assists for steering and braking, and dozens of other improvements. Still, the basic principles of the internal combustion engine, four wheels, and an enclosed carriage for passengers are the same as when Henry Ford brought out the Model T.

One might say the same thing about higher education today. The physical campus, the lecture hall, and the textbook haven't really changed much in a century, despite the addition of computerized systems, ergonomically designed classrooms, and any number of other improvements.

Disruptive innovations, on the other hand, are discontinuous, revolutionary creations that significantly alter the existing landscape and its systems by disrupting "the bigger-and-better cycle by bringing to market a product or service that is not as good as the best traditional offerings but is more affordable and easier to use" (Christensen & Eyring, 2011, p. xxiv). As Christensen and Eyring (2011) pointed out, a disruptive innovation is in competition with the product or service it disrupts. Typically, existing providers under-estimate its potential and incorrectly assume their clientele will not be interested.

In their initial stages, disruptive innovations are not as good as what they replace. For instance, digital photography was clearly inferior to film in its first few years. Eastman Kodak failed to see the full potential of the digital revolution that was coming and how deeply it would erode its dominant position in the photographic film industry, eventually causing the company to declare bankruptcy.

When a disruptive innovation occurs, over time two things begin to happen. First, new customers enter the market. Some are those who could not access or afford

A disruptive innovation is in competition with the product or service it disrupts.

what was previously offered, while others see an opportunity and embrace the disruption, becoming trendsetters. Second, as more and more customers enter the market, new advances (sustaining innovations) make the disruptive offering increasingly attractive. As the disruptive innovation continues to evolve through its own sustaining innovations, it becomes a serious competitor and threat to those who hold on to the past (Christensen & Eyring, 2011). Eventually, the disruptive innovation reaches a tipping point of acceptance and becomes a mainstream offering. The previous product or service may disappear completely or become highly marginalized. The increasingly refined cell phone camera serves as an outstanding example of how disruptive digital technology eliminated the need for film and film cameras; through sustaining innovations, the digital camera evolved so completely that through its tiny lens one can take photos or create videos with sound.

Innovation Is About Creating Value for a Customer

Innovation means creating a commercial value for some beneficiary. That value is based on the wants, needs, and aspirations of the customer. That value may lie in creating greater utility, improving quality, increasing convenience, or lowering cost. Sometimes, the innovation effectively "creates" a need by providing something that the customer didn't know was possible. The wireless smartphone is an example of something that was new 20 years ago that we now can't imagine life without. This is true even though a smartphone costs much more than a phone that just makes phone calls.

For universities and colleges, the principal beneficiary of an improved value proposition is the student. Innovations that will provide new value might bring about lower cost, greater access, enhanced convenience, alternative opportunities, and improved instruction. All of these can lead to a greater likelihood of attaining a degree, shorter time to graduation, or improved employment opportunities.

Ignoring pent-up demand for innovation that improves value can lead to serious consequences. One of the most urgent areas for innovation is in making college more affordable. The financial elasticity of the student market in response to tuition and fee increases has come about by deferring the cost—assuming bigger student loans, larger parent contributions, and additional hours of part-time employment. For many students, passing more costs on to the consumer has reached its limit. Many voices are now warning higher education that it cannot succeed by continuously raising tuition and fees in order to offset diminishing state support, declining enrollments, and increased operating costs.

One of the most urgent areas for innovation is in making college more affordable.

Sustaining innovation to maintain the status quo is not a substitute for making the disruptive leap to something new. Higher education institutions have evolved by emulating, imitating, and competing with each other. As a result, institutions have become more alike than different. Competition for students has intensified as the available pool has stabilized. Compounding the problem of growing enrollment is the fact that at many institutions the loss of students between the first and second years is up to 45%, which means the number of this year's freshmen will have to be replaced before enrollment numbers can be increased. Many students who have dropped out are reluctant to reenter the traditional university or college model, searching instead for a more viable approach to further their education. Technological innovations are creating alternative approaches to learning that will attract not only students who have dropped out, but also others who are interested in those alternative learning opportunities.

Traditional institutions that survive will do so by retaining their best features while responding to and incorporating disruptive innovations into their delivery of instruction and the student experience. Christensen and Eyring (2011) are correct in their observation that "in the past, teaching was difficult to disrupt because its human qualities couldn't be replaced" (p. xi). But this is no longer the case, because "teaching will be disruptable as online learning technology improves and shifts the competitive focus from a teacher's credentials or an institution's prestige to what students actually [or want to] learn" (Christensen & Eyring, 2011, p. xi).

> *Traditional institutions that survive will do so by retaining their best features while responding to and incorporating disruptive innovations.*

AN EXAMPLE OF DISRUPTIVE INNOVATION: THE POST OFFICE

To see how disruptive and sustaining innovations can change the world, one need look no further than the U.S. Postal Service. From the moment that Benjamin Franklin assumed the title of the first postmaster general in 1775, the post office held a virtual monopoly on a vital form of communication: the physical transportation of written documents. The means of transport was continually improved. Letters moved first by horseback, then by stagecoach and train, then by truck and airplane. Thousands of workers were needed to sort, transport, and deliver the mail.

Individuals and businesses relied on the post office for virtually all written communication for nearly 200 years. Then something came along that would disrupt this business model profoundly. That something was the *idea* of the electronic transmission of documents coupled with the digital capability to do so.

Although the technology of sending the image of a document over a wire had been around for a long time, the first commercially viable fax machines were not introduced until the early 1970s. These devices could send a duplicate of any written document over conventional telephone wires in a matter of minutes. Xerox began to sell tens of thousands of these machines and soon others did, too. Slowly, the adoption of this technology began to grow and replace the letters that businesses sent to each other. Still, consumers didn't have fax machines in their homes and the impact on the post office was low. Even when later innovations created devices that combined phone, printing, scanning, and fax capabilities in a multipurpose machine, there was no real threat to the mail as it had been known.

In the 1980s and 1990s, another wave of disruptive innovation happened with the simultaneous growth of the personal computer and the Internet. The electronic transmission of documents took an enormous leap forward with e-mail. The transmission of documents via the Internet became instantaneous and virtually free. The value of reduced cost and increased convenience was gained, in exchange for the loss of the charm of getting a handwritten letter in the mail.

Today, the U.S. Postal Service is struggling. It cannot function without generous government subsidies. It likely will continue to

The ultimate lesson is that wherever there is a monopoly that can be disrupted by innovation, organizations must learn to innovate themselves.

exist in some form, helped ironically by the demand for package delivery created by Internet merchants. Even in that, it must compete with shipping and logistics companies, such as FedEx and UPS, to create value. The ultimate lesson is that wherever there is a monopoly that can be disrupted by innovation, organizations must learn to innovate themselves. That the post office never made a serious foray into providing electronic mail is a serious indictment of its complacency in the face of innovation.

DISRUPTIVE INNOVATION DOES NOT TAKE PRISONERS, IT ELIMINATES THEM

The belief that certain financial institutions were too big to fail proved the undoing of the U.S. economy during the global economic decline in the late 2000s decade, when we experienced the Great Recession. The American landscape is also littered with businesses and whole industries that were thought too big to fail, but that did fail when their customers went elsewhere to take advantage of cheaper or improved services offered by innovative competitors. Higher education institutions are not exempt from this trend. Technology has altered the centuries-old traditional knowledge transfer process that requires campus settings, teachers in classrooms, libraries and living accommodations, and an entire set of attendant site-based amenities. Those that resist innovation and change will find themselves overwhelmed by it.

Innovation is the key to success for organizations that wish to adapt and thrive while confronting unpredictable, chaotic, and volatile times. Perilously, universities and colleges are not by nature innovative organisms. Even when institutions understand that the past is no longer a predictor of the future, they don't know how to behave and, ironically, seem unwilling or unable to learn. Tradition; established interests among faculty, staff, and administrators; and attitudes that value stability over change dominate academic thinking and behavior.

When changes in higher education have occurred, they have been mostly reactive and often begrudgingly absorbed by institutions. As a result, management in academia resembles the industrial corporate model with centralized control and functional silos. Faculty members have given up autonomy for security by becoming unionized. Institutional loyalties have been displaced by the guarding of self- and departmental interests, college and divisional boundaries, and the promulgating of policies and procedures that make responding to innovation and change very difficult. These developments have made the university less flexible

> *Even when institutions understand that the past is no longer a predictor of the future, they don't know how to behave and, ironically, seem unwilling or unable to learn.*

and less adaptive as it faces today's forces of change and the increasing turbulence they will bring tomorrow.

Some of the strongest resisters are powerful alumni, donors, and other constituents who are strongly connected to the institution's past and wish to preserve the traditions and privileges that tie them to the present. If an institution is to survive and thrive, its leaders must be willing to embrace change through sustaining or disruptive innovations in the institution's way of life.

ATTITUDES ON INNOVATION: FACULTY AND ADMINISTRATORS SEE THE FUTURE DIFFERENTLY

The future is continually unfolding in the present. The challenges and opportunities of the next 5, 10, or 20 years are visible today—if we have the wisdom to see them. The present is not the future, but the seeds of the future are in the present.

The seeds of disruptive innovations are sometimes recognizable, but how they will play out remains undetermined. They do not define the future, but they can become tools for reshaping it to our liking. As their inherent possibilities are recognized and utilized, the potential for further change is unleashed. This occurs because once the disruptive innovations are implemented, the sustaining innovations that follow keep compounding their impact.

"Attitudes on Innovation: How College Leaders and Faculty See the Issue of Higher Education," a survey conducted by *The Chronicle of Higher Education* (Selingo, 2013), provided several interesting and useful insights:

✳ "Faculty members are generally pessimistic about the direction of higher education in the United States while presidents are generally optimistic." (p. 1)

✳ Both think that the "rank of the U.S. higher education position in the world is likely to decline in the next ten years." (p. 1)

✳ Both think that faculty should be the drivers of innovation, but presidents don't see faculty as being in this role currently, which "raises the question of how to successfully engage faculty involved in driving innovation." (p. 1)

✳ Both "see blended learning, adaptive learning and interactive technology as the most promising aspects of innovation." (p. 1)

✳ Both "are suspicious of ideas that threaten the status quo or the business model of higher education, such as competency-based degrees, prior learning assessments, open education resources and massive open online courses." (p. 1)

✳ Both agree that "discussions on innovation should be around changes to the teaching-learning model, but current discussions are instead focused on technology and cost cutting." (p. 1)

✳ Both "agree that hybrid courses are better than online-only courses, but they disagree on whether hybrid learning provides equal value compared to the traditional classroom" (p. 1). However, faculty think the value is not equal; presidents think it is.

These findings are clearly disheartening for anyone who hopes that the energy for implementing sustaining innovation will come easily, or at all, from within the walls of the higher education establishment. If it does come from internal pressure, it will be driven by declining enrollments, student resistance to increased tuition and fees, and/or reduced government financial support, any of which will necessitate eliminating academic courses, student services, and employees.

The great irony is that disruptive innovations, mostly generated by technological advances, do not have to meet monumental resistance and passive-aggressive efforts as they affect campuses. They can be constructively harnessed to make a positive difference *if* college and university leaders take a different approach in how they respond to them. As a result, the most pressing issue facing college and university executives is how to lead the institution in preparing its members to be flexible integrators of innovation and nimble agents of change.

> *The great irony is that disruptive innovations, mostly generated by technological advances, do not have to meet monumental resistance.*

College and university leaders must think of innovation, not as a static process, but as a dynamic one. Whether the innovations they are encountering are a product, process, theory, idea, or a composite of these, the early stages of impact and development require nurturing. College and university leaders need to prevent their institutions from being held hostage to individual or group pressures for preserving the past or the present without open and forthright evaluation of the possible unintended consequences of the innovation. Employees from all institutional levels—whether they have formal or informal power or are faculty, professional staff, support staff, or administrators—need to understand the consequences faced by other sectors that have resisted disruptive innovations. They also need to understand how they can respond affirmatively and create new ways to lead and participate in innovation and change without diluting cherished values, professional practices, and best traditions.

CLOUD STATE UNIVERSITY IS JUST AROUND THE CORNER

In some ways, the future has already arrived as disruptive innovation approaches the tipping point in higher education. Current innovations (such as massive open online courses, online learning, hybrid curricula, and flipped classrooms) are simply the precursors of what the future will be like. If, rather than trying to hold back change, higher education institutions can seize the innovative initiative to invent "Cloud State University," bringing with them their governing boards and organizations as well as accrediting and professional

> *In some ways, the future has already arrived as disruptive innovation approaches the tipping point in higher education.*

associations, they will not have to worry about transferring control of the future of the educational franchise to others who seek entrepreneurial opportunities.

Many different kinds of stakeholders are waiting for Cloud State University. The growing national discontent with educational costs and outcomes is creating pressure for innovation and change. This is reflected in increased federal government involvement in educational policy, rules, regulations, and funding. Employers want graduates who are better prepared to enter the changing world of work. State governors and legislatures are looking for ways of making even greater reductions in higher education funding while increasing accountability. Finally, large numbers of students do not graduate and yet leave with large student debt.

> *The value proposition of Cloud State University will be that it can provide a learning experience that will match each individual student's capabilities, needs, and wants.*

The biggest task for higher education is to reshape the way it delivers the learning experience and to harness the innovations that will make this happen. The value proposition of Cloud State University will be that it can provide a learning experience that will match each individual student's capabilities, needs, and wants whether that student is in residence on campus, coming to a satellite facility, learning online, or using some combination of these modalities. The one thing we can anticipate about Cloud University is that it will learn, from the information it collects and from the patterns the students exhibit, how best to help them achieve their stated goals.

All one has to do is to become familiar with Google, Facebook, Amazon, and a few other modern-day companies to realize that their enormous success in creating, growing, and sustaining customer relationships is built on their intimate knowledge of who their customers are, what they like and do, and where/when/with whom they do it. Just by being members of modern society, today's students are being taught to expect service providers to initiate contact to inform them about routine matters, new products, and other opportunities they should consider, and in turn solicit information on how the service provider can be of additional assistance. Expectations set by the businesses that are analyzing big data to interactively market and serve their customers are being transferred to all other sectors, including higher education. When consumers evaluate customer service from higher education, they measure their experience against the best of what they have experienced elsewhere. Students are no exception; Google, Facebook, and Amazon set the new standard for customer service.

THINK OF INNOVATION AS AN "IF–THEN" STATEMENT THAT GENERATES SOLUTIONS

Randall S. Wright (2012) stated that "too many executives confuse what an innovation is with what an innovation would do for them if they had one" (p. 96). His solution is to think of innovation as an if–then argument. He proposed that "all true innovations are arguments ... composed of three elements: a proposition and conclusion linked by an inference" (p. 95). He further stated that "arguments can be expressed as if–then statements: *if* we agree to a proposition being true . . . *then* we can infer a conclusion" (p. 95). He noted that "innovation conclusions are always about the human experience, and of this, they are usually about empowerment" (p. 95).

The *ifs* are what you do—the innovations; the *thens* are the outcomes—what the innovation achieves. Doing what empowers humans combined with operational excellence is the essence of innovation. It is the *thens* that reveal the utility of innovation, giving it value. Leaders of innovation must always clearly see the *thens,* which are the true measure of the worth of the innovation. Henry Ford's genius was not in building the first car or the first assembly line. It was in connecting the two disparate ideas and giving them utility for mass production, along with paying his workers enough so they could afford to buy his product. Wright (2012) pointed out that the crux of the innovation process is the *thens* that are the drivers of demand. Results emanate from empowering people. Wright (2012) quoted Henry Ford's if–then statement that if I "build a car for the great multitude . . .[then] no man making a good salary will be unable to own one—and enjoy with his family the blessing of hours of pleasure in God's great open spaces" (p. 95).

When preparing if–then statements, it is helpful to answer the following questions to form the foundation for doing so:

> *The ifs are what you do—the innovations; the thens are the outcomes—what the innovation achieves.*

* What will be the CSAO's specific role in leading innovation in the division of student affairs?

* On what specific areas (programs, activities, or services) will innovation be focused?

* How will divisional innovative capabilities be defined, organized, measured, and managed?

* What resources will be needed and how will they be financed?

* What means will be used to communicate the innovation's intended impact?

* What changes will be required in existing structures, policies, and procedures in the student affairs division?

* How will the innovation influence employee interactions and relationships?

* What new skills will be required for managers, supervisors, and staff?

* What training will be available to help develop them?

* How will others who will be affected by the innovation be integrated into the process?

* How will achievements be recognized and rewarded?

* What strategies will be needed for creating and achieving constructive, win–win solutions for their implementation?

* What will empower employees to achieve the planned results while they are confronted with people and forces trying to maintain the status quo?

Perhaps the most important impact that innovation makes on organizational systems is that it requires everyone's involvement to create and implement it. That innovation depends upon extremely talented individuals is an outmoded idea. "Actual evidence points elsewhere. It turns out disciplined teams using effective methods get results 10, even 20 *times* better than current global norms" (Keeley, Pikkel, Quinn, & Walters, 2013, p. 8).

Innovation is a team sport. Those who want to succeed at it must learn to master its skills. With practice, everyone can become better at innovating.

References

Christensen, C. M., & Eyring, H. J. (2011). *The innovative university: Changing the DNA of higher education from the inside out.* San Francisco, CA: Jossey-Bass.

Keeley, L. P., Pikkel, R., Quinn, H., & Walters, H. (2013). *Ten types of innovation: The discipline of building breakthroughs.* Hoboken, NJ: Wiley.

Selingo, J. J. (2013). *Attitudes on innovation: How college leaders and faculty see the key issues facing higher education.* Retrieved from *The Chronicle of Higher Education* website: http://results.chronicle.com/ InnovationSurvey2013_Adobe

Wright, R. S. (2012, March 20). Why innovations are arguments. *MIT Sloan Management Review*, pp. 95–96.

CHAPTER 4

Making Student Affairs the Hub of Innovation

Laurence N. Smith and Albert B. Blixt

It is ironic that the student affairs function is becoming increasingly vulnerable on some campuses, just when it should be an institution's most valuable asset for dealing with the *ifs–thens* of both sustaining and disruptive innovations discussed in Chapter 3. The problem is that chief student affairs officers (CSAOs) do not seem to have picked up on this, and neither have others in their institutions.

CSAOs already have both accountability and responsibility for implementing the *ifs* that will empower students as well as create operational excellence. The out-of-class territory is a large domain in which to be creative and innovative. But instead of organizing and aligning student affairs resources to make a significant difference, CSAOs seem to remain stuck in a conceptual industrial model that diminishes their effectiveness. The administrative structure of student affairs divisions may vary from one institution to another, but at the core is a largely bureaucratic arrangement—administrative silos, with hierarchical reporting relationships and functionally focused departments. Even more frustrating in the innovation and change processes is the fact that employees are more focused on sustaining the boundaries of their administrative units instead of focusing on the well-being and future of the institution.

Of course, there are many examples of collaboration that cut across administrative lines, bringing people from within the division of student affairs together with others from throughout the institution. However, collaboration is usually constricted because it is viewed through the political lenses of the institution and moderated by protecting self-interest. In the best of situations, where this does not occur, collaboration is limited by conflicting demands of other work commitments and time. Even finding time to collaborate is a difficult task as calendars need to be juggled to accommodate team member schedules. And for many team members meetings represent the call for miraculous last-minute effort to do the work they have committed to perform. It has been said that when it comes to committee assignments, as well as other commitments, if it were not for the last minute nothing would get done!

However, by the very nature of their leadership role and administrative purview, CSAOs have the freedom to create sustaining innovations to improve not only their own domain, but also the student experience. Much of student affairs work is transactional and requires a well-trained and dedicated staff. Fortunately, new technologies provide for automated, 24/7 transactional services and access that, when implemented, can release staff from routine tasks to render higher-level, personalized assistance or launch new projects. CSAOs also have both the responsibility and the opportunity to anticipate and respond to the intensifying disruptive innovations

> *CSAOs have the freedom to create sustaining innovations to improve not only their own domain, but also the student experience.*

that confront higher education and challenge student affairs as well as faculty and other areas of the institution.

EIGHT STEPS FOR LEADING INNOVATION

The steps below provide a broad outline of how to transform the division of student affairs into a leader and producer of innovation and change.

1. **Create an Innovation Hub.** The most important effort that CSAOs can undertake is to develop a Student Affairs Innovation Hub within the student affairs division that will discover sustaining innovations and harness the power of disruptive innovations to create new programs, services, and activities that will inspire and engage all students to achieve their educational goals.[1]

---

[1] "All students" implies not only the traditional student who wants an on-campus living experience, but also transfer students; graduate and professional students; hybrid learners who attend on-campus courses and also take online courses; and online learners.

Creating a Student Affairs Innovation Hub within the division of student affairs will require the CSAO's unconditional initial support and strong commitment to the success of the innovation process. The CSAO must be an active player in the innovation process. Leadership *cannot* be delegated or the process will not succeed. The CSAO must be the convener and chair of the Innovation Hub even if its daily operations are delegated to others.

2. **Create an Innovation Team to staff the Innovation Hub.** This is a small group of staff whose members are dedicated to the goals and objectives of the Innovation Hub and who have the competency to achieve its goals. Innovation Team membership cannot be an add-on responsibility but must be made an integral component of the person's accountability, duties, responsibilities, and evaluation. These individuals must have time to devote to this work.

Although the Innovation Team must be populated with division of student affairs members, others from within the institution's faculty, administration, alumni, or community can also be included. The team will best function with a small number of core team members; others should be appointed as consultants and be involved as needed.

The Innovation Team needs to be divided into two work groups: a Sustaining Innovation Work Group and a Disruptive Innovation Work Group, since each requires a very different approach. However, even though they have divergent focuses, the groups must work together to share their findings and consult with one another.

The Sustaining Innovation Work Group should focus on innovations that will improve what is currently in place at the institution. The sustaining innovation process will identify and analyze what the real problems are,

Creating a Student Affairs Innovation Hub within the division of student affairs will require the CSAO's unconditional initial support

their root causes, who will be affected by the sustaining innovation, and what the innovation's end results will be (the *ifs–thens* of innovation). The work group will identify the processes, programs, and services that can be conducted more effectively and efficiently, which will then allow them to determine what innovations will be useful in attaining the desired objective. This group will need to have the clear backing of senior leaders because it is likely to find resistance as it investigates and analyzes the status quo—something that always makes people nervous.

The Disruptive Innovation Work Group should identify emerging opportunities and apply them to transform the areas of concern. It is not necessarily the job of this work group to create disruptive innovations. This group will scan the horizon continually to identify potentially disruptive developments and ways to anticipate their impact on the division and the university as a whole. This group will be

Team members should be appointed because they have the interest, commitment, background, and skills for making the Innovation Hub successful.

critical in helping the CSAO identify longer-term strategic trends before they are apparent to others.

Team members should be appointed because they have the interest, commitment, background, and skills for making the Innovation Hub successful. Opportunities for further training to enhance skills should be provided as needed. Likewise, internal and external consultants to each of the two work groups should include appointees from disciplines that can provide the analysis, interpretation, and recommendations necessary for transforming innovations into action.

3. **Define the Innovation Team's roles and responsibilities.** The team's charter and charge should clearly state that it is advisory to the CSAO. Team members and consultants need to have a clear understanding that they are not on the Innovation Team as representatives of their respective areas but as valued resources for achieving desired results from both sustaining and disruptive innovation opportunities. The charter should set out the purposes of the team, its goals, and its authority. Specific deliverables and timetables should be determined. There should also be a provision for evaluation of the team's performance on at least an annual basis that can include a "sunset" provision for potential

dissolution of the team or rechartering. The more inclusive the Innovation Team, the more successful it will be in achieving results. Rotating people on and off the team from time to time is an outstanding process to make sure that the Innovation Hub stays in touch with the work of the division and the changing nature of the forces of change and the student body.

4. **Educate division staff about innovation and the Hub's role.** The first job of the Student Affairs Innovation Hub is to educate all division members about innovation, the innovative process, and the hub's role. All division staff members need to be engaged in active learning about innovation, how it can be designed and applied. They must understand the differences between sustaining and disruptive innovations, and how they are currently affecting higher education not only in the United States but also internationally. As the division pursues becoming a learning community on innovation, initial resistance will melt away and excitement for creating innovation will take its place. If there are experts in innovation on the institution's faculty, inviting them to share their knowledge with the division's learning community will build strong supporters outside the division and positive buzz about the effort.

> *The first job of the Student Affairs Innovation Hub is to educate all division members about innovation.*

Although specific teams drive innovation, good ideas can come from anywhere, so everyone needs to feel involved in the process. However, a clear understanding of the innovation process and the Hub's role must convey that its focus is on innovations that will enhance the mission and best achieve the vision of the division, and of course the institution.

It is important to note that although the traditional approach of involving staff in brainstorming sessions to identify creative ideas and innovations has found its way into standard practice, the process may be more effective for political purposes (i.e., creating "buy-in") than for generating fresh ideas and useful innovations. This is not to say that brainstorming with large groups of people is not useful, but for the purposes of being innovative, evidence suggests that this technique does not, by itself, lead to better outcomes (Keeley, Pikkel, Quinn, & Walters, 2013).

5. **Demonstrate visible leadership as CSAO.** As Innovation Team members immerse themselves in the process, they will become more invested and excited about what they are doing. They will be motivated by what their work means for the future of the division, the students it serves, and their own professional development and future options. During this period, the CSAO's leading and guiding presence, strong and nurturing encouragement, and deep interest will be key to the team's energy, pursuits, and results. At the beginning, the team's focus should be germane to

initiatives, programs, services, and activities within the division's role and scope.

The Innovation Hub should be utilized as a way to build alliances across the institution. Traditionally, CSAOs have viewed the academic areas of the institution as their natural partners. This view has not always been reciprocated and is often misunderstood. In-classroom and out-of-classroom experiences are not opposite sides of the same coin. Each provides unique opportunities to prepare students for personal and professional life experiences. It may be that the most

> *The Innovation Hub should be utilized as a way to build alliances across the institution.*

important institutional allies for student affairs in the innovation process are not only faculty and academic administrators, but also those who are in the institution's leadership, administration, and service areas as well as alumni and friends of the school.

As the leader, the CSAO must be willing to take the initiative. The best way to kill off the Innovation Hub or even just an innovative effort is first to seek permission to pursue it and second to make other institutional officers feel they need to be supportive to make it work. (See Chapter 13 for more on creating the Innovation Hub.) The learning activities in Step 2 should have helped reduce resistance. Even if it hasn't removed all resistance, Step 2 provides a common

Because people support what they help to create, it is important to create interventions that involve those who could be affected by these deliberations.

understanding regarding the need to adopt innovative solutions and the processes for doing so.

The CSAO must make sure that people are informed, involved, and talking to each other. Open communication is critical and gaining consensus is important. Because people support what they help to create, it is important to create interventions that involve those who could be affected by these deliberations. Consensus does not need to be unanimous, but it relies on there being more support than not.

6. **Create a data-driven attitude.** Using data to direct action requires charging the Sustaining Innovation Work Group with the responsibility for converting new and existing data into decision-making tools. Most institutions have centralized information technology systems that can be used for data management activities, accessing information about students that has already been collected and stored. Most data goes untapped when it should be used for analyzing, interpreting, and recommending solutions to be considered in institutional decision making.

   The Sustaining Innovation Work Group also needs to identify successful innovation practices at other higher education institutions, health organizations, and businesses that collect information about their customers, to identify options for creating a best-in-class data management model. What are called best practices should be studied for the options they offer and not as practices to be blindly transplanted into another institution.

It is worth noting that as the ease of collecting and storing data has increased, the storage cost has decreased significantly. However, data that cannot be easily accessed, analyzed, and converted into a useful tool for decision making are a lost opportunity. Understanding data about the impediments and drivers that determine student enrollment decisions, academic performance, and the likelihood of retention to graduation is a critical innovative component for designing admissions outreach, academic advising, and related support services. Determining accurate and specific cause and effect is an essential ingredient for designing innovations that will produce desired results.

The common wisdom that guides much institutional decision making is often wrong. Just because there is agreement about something doesn't mean that it is correct. As Michael Mauboussin, author of "The True Measure of Success," pointed out, "People's deep confidence in their judgments and abilities is often at odds with reality"

> *Determining accurate and specific cause and effect is an essential ingredient for designing innovations that will produce desired results.*

(p. 49). He cautioned further that "it's surprising how often people assign the wrong cause to an outcome," and noted that, "this failure results from an innate desire to find cause and effect in every situation—to create a narrative that explains how events are linked even when they're not" (p. 52). This might help explain why, after several decades of attempting to reverse the exceptionally high attrition rate of undergraduate students, universities and colleges have not been able to do so despite special campus initiatives promoted by consultants, conferences, and common campus wisdom.

Disruptive Innovation Work Group members need to be charged with collecting and investigating the wide array of information about emerging disruptive innovations, and then to summarize current thinking about the impact on higher education in general, and students in particular. Even though much of the information about disruptive innovation is in a formative stage, it is essential to begin planning for its impact. This information also needs to be collected, sorted, analyzed, and reported so that student affairs discussions can be focused and productive and lead to decisions on how to respond.

7. **Ask the right questions.** Keeley, Pikkel, Quinn, and Walters (2013) presented a breakthrough approach to innovation in the corporate world that also has much to say to higher education. Their section on "What to Ask; Where to Focus" offers an excellent framework for student affairs to pursue in its search for innovations that really will make a

difference. Their advice: "Be conscious about the decisions you're making—and understand the way they may evolve over time. After all, innovation should never be static; even the best innovations evolve over time" (p. 184).

The following suggestions are not necessarily sequential. They can be applied simultaneously to different aspects of the division's work. The authors present these insights and activities to "help imagine, develop and sustain new innovation capabilities" (Keeley, Pikkel, Quinn, & Walters, 2013, p. 185). For ease in reading, they are paraphrased and modified to reflect their application for student affairs and other institutional areas:

* ***Rethink.*** Rethink what your students need, understand what they hate about their experience with the programs, activities, services, policies, and procedures at your institution and especially with student affairs and services. What novel offerings can you add that are not the norm within student affairs now? How can you integrate these smoothly and painlessly (for the division, institution, and your students)?

* ***Reimagine.*** Reimagine how your leadership as CSAO and the division of student affairs might actually change their lives. What about the status quo is just stupid at the core? What baffles students and others, wastes their time, or is just so insanely difficult that they don't do it?

* *Reframe.* How might you enlarge or reinvent the category? It's often the case that (paradoxically) by making the problem bigger you can usefully make it simpler and important in fresh ways.

* *Engage.* What bold student promise would be startling and newsworthy? Think of providing something no other college or university now offers, and then figure out how you can deliver it with a guarantee.

* *Extend.* Who are your ideal students? Be as expansive as possible. Ideally your ecosystem should make it possible for many students to prosper. How can your way become the easiest way for anyone to achieve outstanding success in the near future?

* *Expand.* Who will do what? What gives you as CSAO the right to be the central player in the innovation endeavor? What do you have to do to ensure that you are paving the way to stake this territory as yours? (Keeley, Pikkel, Quinn, & Walters, 2013, p. 185).

Remember: Focus on the division of student affairs, for which you have accountability and responsibility! As your innovations for the division take hold and prove successful, you can then explore your leadership role in helping other institutional areas also become truly innovative.

8. **Separate innovation from implementation.** Innovators are not necessarily change agents, and change agents are not necessarily innovators. Each of these areas requires separate,

dedicated, and specialized approaches in order to flourish. Part of the transfer process from paper to practice requires an operational shift that includes answering two vital questions: (1) What will be changed? (2) How do we have to change to make it happen? Chapter 8, "The CSAO as Change Champion," suggests a process for transforming innovations from concepts into being.

> *Innovators are not necessarily change agents, and change agents are not necessarily innovators.*

In a relay race, two runners run together while they pass the baton. Passing an innovation from the Innovation Team to a Change Team requires running together as well. It is during this transition period that the two questions posed above ultimately must be answered.

THE VALUES THAT FOSTER INNOVATION

Breakthrough innovations don't just happen. They come about from the way people think and from the values that guide their actions. Whether you call it a culture of innovation or an innovative mindset, the CSAO must make certain that select core principles guide the thoughts of everyone working in student affairs. This begins with the CSAO practicing these values and leading by example. Among the most important values are:

✴ **Curiosity.** This is where innovation begins. Be curious about what you know and what you don't know. Pay attention to what is happening, not only in higher education but also in the world. Encourage others to do the same. Be curious about the literature of innovation and the trends and developments that affect higher education. Read widely—you never know where new ideas will come from. Don't be afraid of learning things that challenge what you think you know now. It is the collision of ideas or the unexpected intersection of disparate ideas that generates breakthroughs.

✴ **Imagination.** Everybody has imagination, but it is important that your imagination emerges from your curiosity. Practice being playful with a purpose. Imagine something wonderful that will help students even if it seems impossible or impractical at the moment. Tell your inner critic to take the day off. Idea generation and creativity provide the raw material for innovation. With lots of ideas, you have choices to try and to learn from.

✴ **Courage.** Be willing to be wrong in the pursuit of what's right, which in this case is to ensure that your institution is helping students succeed in ways that will surprise and please them. You also need to instill courage in your staff by letting them take intelligent risks in search of better answers. When something doesn't work, don't shoot the messenger; ask "What can we learn from this?" and move on. Taking a calculated risk might not always work out as intended, but failing is part of the innovation process. No one is immune from failure. What is important to focus on is not the failure, but how to land on your feet, regroup, and move forward.

* **Patience.** Innovation is sometimes messy and frustrating. Getting people involved in collaborative exploration takes time but will yield better results than imposing something that worked somewhere else but may not work here. Of course, you need to measure results and encourage productivity. Just don't mistake speed for efficiency. Remember, if you are not a patient person, at least try to look patient. It will make an important difference.

* **Persistence.** Make innovation a priority and do not let your staff assume that this is just another "flavor of the month" initiative that will soon fade. Innovation and adaptability should be central to your management philosophy. Make sure your direct reports and those of your staff also embrace this philosophy.

REFERENCES

Keeley, L. P., Pikkel, R., Quinn, H., & Walters, H. (2013). *Ten types of innovation: The discipline of building breakthroughs.* Hoboken, NJ: Wiley.

Mauboussin, M. J. (2012, October). The true measures of success. *Harvard Business Review*, pp. 46–56.

CHAPTER 5

The CSAO and the "Secret" Formula for Change

Albert B. Blixt and Laurence N. Smith

Earlier chapters in this book outlined the knowledge, skills, and attitudes that chief student affairs officers (CSAOs) need to carry out their leadership responsibilities and how they can foster innovation in the institutional setting. In referring to leading change, we mean designing and executing a planned response that enables an organization to be more effective in responding to internal and external circumstances. This chapter and the three that follow continue that discussion by describing what student affairs leaders need to know about systemic transformational change and how to achieve it.

HOW SYSTEMIC TRANSFORMATIONAL CHANGE
IS DIFFERENT FROM OTHER KINDS OF CHANGE

Change takes place at different levels and degrees. Some changes are local and some are systemic. Some changes are intended to sustain the system and some are intended to alter it dramatically. All of these kinds of changes are important and each has challenges of its own. It is important for the student affairs executive to recognize these different kinds of change and to know how to bring them about effectively.

The institution as it is can deal with some change. This is the kind of change that happens when a new semester begins, when a new budget or procedure is adopted, or when there is a change in personnel. This may include changes that seek to improve on existing results. These are transactional or incremental changes. They are about making adjustments to the status quo or fixing a problem. Most of the time, these can be managed without making any fundamental changes to the organization or its culture. For the CSAO, these changes are part of "business as usual" and most of the work can be delegated to subordinates.

Systemic changes are ones that have an impact on multiple levels and functions and span organizational boundaries. Transformational changes require alteration of the processes, structures, and daily work of the

> *Transformational changes require alteration of the processes, structures, and daily work of the organization in ways that are pretty fundamental.*

organization in ways that are pretty fundamental. This kind of change forces people out of their comfort zones and can provoke passive and active resistance. That is what makes the leader's role so essential.

UNDERSTANDING THE "SECRET" DYNAMICS OF CHANGE: THE DVF FORMULA

Have you wondered why some change efforts succeed and others fail? To succeed, real transformational change efforts must account for the combination of three critical factors that, although not really a secret, are mostly unknown to many leaders. The dynamics of bringing about change in an organization are explained by the DVF Formula[1] (Beckhard & Harris, 1987; Dannemiller Tyson Associates, 2000), as illustrated in Figure 5.1.

Figure 5.1. *The DVF Formula for Change*

$$D \times V \times F > R$$

D = **Dissatisfaction** with the current situation that creates a sense of urgency

V = **Vision** of the future that is positive and compelling

F = **First steps** in the direction of the vision

R = **Resistance** to change

Note. Adapted from Dannemiller Tyson Associates, 2000, p. 16. Reprinted with permission.

---

[1] The DVF Formula, also known as the DxVxF>R Model, was originally based on the work of Richard Beckhard and Reuben Harris (1987). It was refined and expanded by Kathleen Dannemiller and her partners at Dannemiller Tyson Associates, including Albert B. Blixt.

This formula is based on the idea that an organization will tend to continue to operate in the same way unless there is a force that causes it to change. The tendency to continue is called Resistance (R) and is best understood as a form of inertia that keeps things moving in the same direction; organizations are remarkably persistent in maintaining the status quo. In order to overcome that resistance, the formula states that three factors need to be present.

First, each individual and the organization as a whole must share a common database of Dissatisfaction (D) with the current situation. The leader's job is to help people have enough information to see the big picture case for change and appreciate the frustrations and aspirations held by others. Dissatisfaction comes from knowing more about the situation and becoming convinced that continuing as we have been is unacceptable. This creates a willingness to change and a sense of urgency. The leader needs to do what is necessary to get people talking to each other and sharing information to create that sense of urgency.

> *Dissatisfaction comes from knowing more about the situation and becoming convinced that continuing as we have been is unacceptable.*

The second step in creating change is to establish a common Vision (V) of what the organization wants to become in the future. The V describes a vivid and robust picture of what might lie just over the horizon. It provides direction and motivation. A major section of this chapter is devoted to the CSAO's vital role in developing and sharing a vision, whether it is for the institution or the division of student affairs. The final step is to have clear First Steps (F) in the direction of change. It is not enough that people are motivated and aligned in wanting a new preferred future. They must also have a clear path toward that future that gives them direction and lets them know that progress is being made.

The secret of the DVF Formula is that it is an inequality. The product of D, V, and F must be greater than R or nothing will change. If any of those three factors is zero then the product will be zero. Too many leaders shortchange the F when they know they have a problem, spend a lot of time creating a great vision, and then assume that change will happen by itself. Whether you are trying to change a division, a department, or an entire institution, some combination of D, V, and F is needed. It is the combination of factors that matters. If Dissatisfaction is great, then a more modest Vision will be enough to make progress.

It is important to pay attention to all four elements of the formula, including Resistance. Resistance plays an important role because it tells you what may be missing in the plan for change. In general, people resist what they don't understand or what they fear. A wise leader honors resistance by listening and making accommodations where needed.

The leader must see to it that everyone in the organization understands, believes in, and commits to the vision and to achieving it.

The leader must help people see how they can contribute to the vision and succeed in that new picture.

The leader must help people see how they can contribute to the vision and succeed in that new picture. If they can't or won't, it is the leader's job to help them find a new position or leave the organization as diplomatically as possible.

THE CSAO OPERATES AS A CHANGE LEADER AT TWO LEVELS

The CSAO operates at two levels: the institutional and the divisional. These two are intertwined but distinctly different. At the institutional level, the CSAO is part of an executive leadership team helping to develop and implement strategy. At this level, the CSAO has influence but not control. The student affairs executive must work with the president, the provost, and other vice presidents to create a unified approach to student success. The CSAO must have a keen awareness of the importance of cross-functional cooperation to achieve strategic goals and needs political savvy to gain support for his or her proposals. In short, the CSAO must be an effective team player who can gain the respect and trust of peers and superiors.

At the divisional level, the CSAO must be both a leader and a manager. Both are required to effect change. As a leader, the CSAO must be able to articulate and advocate for a vision for the division that supports the strategy of the institution. The leader must be able to make the case for change and help everyone in the division embrace the promise of that vision. As a manager, the CSAO must be able to lay out a roadmap for the change initiative and then engage everyone in the division to bring it to reality.

The best way for the CSAO to be respected as a leader at the institutional level is by demonstrating success in leading the student affairs division. The CSAO typically has a lot of control and is able to have a large impact through the programs and services offered by the division. Learning to lead change in the division of student affairs is a good way to develop leadership skills and to enhance one's reputation with peers and superiors.

> *The best way for the CSAO to be respected as a leader at the institutional level is by demonstrating success in leading the student affairs division.*

The next three chapters will focus on three distinct aspects of successful change leadership:

* Strategic thinking: The leader's role as visionary
* Strategic planning: The leader's role as change architect
* Strategic implementation: The leader's role as change champion

These competencies are all needed if a leader is going to do what is required to move the organization to a new future with the support and commitment of its people.

REFERENCES

Beckhard, R., & Harris, R. T. (1987). *Organizational transitions: Managing complex change* (2nd ed.). Reading, MA: Addison-Wesley.

Dannemiller Tyson Associates. (2000). *Whole-scale change: Unleashing the magic in organizations.* Ann Arbor, MI: Berrett-Koehler.

CHAPTER 6

The CSAO as Visionary

Albert B. Blixt and Laurence N. Smith

Bringing about systemic transformational change begins with vision. You don't have to be a charismatic or heroic leader to help your organization create a vision that will guide and motivate the kind of innovation and positive action you need. Vision is the product of strategic thinking and it follows some simple principles.

VISION IS THE FULCRUM FOR LEVERAGING STRATEGY

The role of vision is at the center of the strategic planning model explored in this chapter (Figure 6.1). This model is a version of the Whole-Scale Change model developed by Dannemiller Tyson Associates (2000).

This model builds on the DVF Formula discussed in Chapter 5, expanding on the ideas of Dissatisfaction, Vision, and First Steps. Each term used in the model evokes a series of questions that helps complete the strategy. Dissatisfaction is based on data (stakeholder needs + internal and external environment) that tells us where the organization is currently in fulfilling its Mission. The Vision is the future picture of success that inspires and guides all action. The Vision points the way to what we need to focus on (Strategic Goals and Objectives) and what First Steps we will take to achieve them. Taken together, the motivation of Dissatisfaction, the direction of Vision, and the action described in First Steps in the direction of the change constitutes a strategy that can drive the adaptive change that is needed.

Vision is the future picture of success that inspires and guides all action.

Figure 6.1. *Strategic Planning Model*

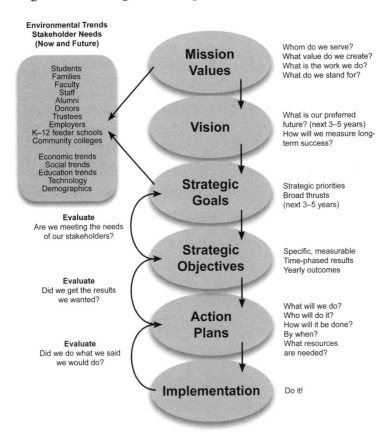

Environmental Trends
Stakeholder Needs
(Now and Future)

Students
Families
Faculty
Staff
Alumni
Donors
Trustees
Employers
K–12 feeder schools
Community colleges

Economic trends
Social trends
Education trends
Technology
Demographics

Mission Values — Whom do we serve? What value do we create? What is the work we do? What do we stand for?

Vision — What is our preferred future? (next 3–5 years) How will we measure long-term success?

Strategic Goals — Strategic priorities Broad thrusts (next 3–5 years)

Strategic Objectives — Specific, measurable Time-phased results Yearly outcomes

Action Plans — What will we do? Who will do it? How will it be done? By when? What resources are needed?

Implementation — Do it!

Evaluate Are we meeting the needs of our stakeholders?

Evaluate Did we get the results we wanted?

Evaluate Did we do what we said we would do?

STRATEGIC TERMS AND THE QUESTIONS THEY EVOKE

Stakeholders: Who are our primary customers whose interests we serve? Who are the others who are counting on our organization for something? Who is needed to contribute to the success of the organization? Who has influence and impact on our organization? Who has the power of "no" whose voices could derail our efforts?

Mission: What is the focus of all value-creating action? What is the short, clear, and compelling statement that inspires people to devote themselves to achieving that purpose?

Values: What are the few rules and principles that govern our behavior even when "the going gets tough"? What really defines us behaviorally? What are our sacred beliefs about our behavior, so that if we violate them we are not suitable to belong?

Vision: What is the future we want to create for this organization? What will it look like if we are living our mission magnificently and truly serving the needs of our stakeholders?

Strategic goals: What are the few priorities that we need to focus on as an organization? What are the broad thrusts where we need to focus in order to move toward our vision? (next 3–5 years)

Strategic objectives: What are the time-phased outcomes of working on our strategic goals? What specific results will we achieve this year? What are the milestones we will use to measure our success?

Note. Adapted from Dannemiller Tyson Associates, 2000, p. 234. Reprinted with permission.

Vision Is About Imagining a Preferred Future

One thing we can be sure of is that we can't know the future. Efforts to examine trends, conduct research, and extrapolate from the past to predict future events will likely be of little value and will lead to a reactive response aimed more at solving the problems of the present than at seeking to influence the future. While it is essential to know about the past and the lessons it teaches, it takes a different kind of thinking to be ready to imagine a future of our own choosing.

Professor Ronald Lippitt (1982) coined the phrase "preferred futuring" to describe the process in this way:

> So the job of <u>preferred futuring</u> requires that we examine the data of the past, the present, and the events, trends, and developments (EDTs) going on around in our world, community, organization, and personal lives. Then we use these data to imagine and envision images of the <u>future that we prefer</u>, not limited by presently perceived frontiers, yet triggered by the realities of the present and emerging technological situation.
>
> Then we take that commitment to preferred and prioritized images and move toward intentional action by preparing a goal-and-action implementation plan which will make optimal use of the human and technological resources of the organization. (p. 185)

Futuring, as described by Lippitt (1982), is the precursor of planning but is something quite different. As we, the authors, have worked with organizational leaders, senior managers, and planning teams on the futuring and planning process, we have been impressed with the variety of ways of thinking and the activities involved in the freedom of futuring and the discipline of planning. Table 6.1 shows how leaders have described the differences.

Table 6.1. *Differences between Futuring and Planning*

Futuring	Planning	Futuring	Planning
Searching	Defining	Open	Committed
Field-oriented	Linear	Qualitative	Quantitative
Comprehensive	Bottom-line	Ambiguous	Certain
Scenarios	Objectives	Forecast	Decide
Intuitive	Systematic	Explore	Map
Hypothesis	Conclusion	Possible	Feasible
Fluid	Disciplined	Open	Committed
Direction	Path	Prefer	Design

Note. Adapted from Lippitt, 1982, p. 186. Reprinted with permission.

One of the great challenges of creating a vision is to generate pictures of possibility without coming to conclusions too quickly. There is an ancient saying that the beginner sees a thousand possibilities while the expert can see only one. The work of the leader is to first open the team to creating possible scenarios and then to come to closure together on the most important priorities.

BEGINNING THE FUTURING AND PLANNING PROCESS: FORMING A "FUTURES WORK GROUP"

Eventually it will be essential to engage people from across the organization in thinking about the future, but it is best to begin with a group of leaders whose commitment and support will be needed to implement the strategy. This can include both formal (positional) and informal (influential) leaders. The purpose of this group will be to develop a draft vision that others can react to while thinking creatively and strategically as a team. The work group might include 10 to 30 individuals who represent different functions at either the divisional or institutional level.

There is an ancient saying that the beginner sees a thousand possibilities while the expert can see only one.

The work group might begin with the president and the cabinet or the chief student affairs officer (CSAO) and direct reports and then be expanded to include other voices that will add perspectives to the work. The charge of this work group will be to study the current situation, identify the challenges and opportunities, and propose a vision statement that is a vivid, realistic, and inspiring picture of the future. The group may also suggest where the organization needs to focus its energy in order to move toward that vision.

The first step for the work group will be to establish a common database of information that will spark their thinking and creativity. Where will this kind of team look for the data it needs to think about the future? The following are some suggestions from Lippitt (1982).

* In our culture we tend to avoid reflecting on our past as an organization in order to gain perspective in thinking about the future. One way to do this is by creating a "history wall" where the life of the organization is divided into decades and group members brainstorm the themes and events of the past by decades. Then the group reflects on the meaning of those themes—as achievements, mistakes, turning points, patterns, important values, breakthrough innovations, etc.

* A second place to look for data for future planning is a review of plans and goals that have been set but not yet fully actualized. Assessing what we said we would do vis-à-vis what we actually did do will be valuable.

* A third familiar source is input from our assessments and surveys of the needs, expectations, and desires of our key constituencies. Student affairs offices often have an abundant supply of this kind of information, although it may need to be formatted and analyzed. It will be helpful to think in advance about what the team really needs to know. For instance, it might be interesting to know how many students were flagged as being at risk by our early alert system (process) but it would be much more useful to know how many of those students received an intervention that actually worked in getting them back on track (outcome).

* A fourth source of data is a review of current operations and achievements. Unfortunately, we tend to focus on what is going wrong and ignore what is going right. Have the group balance this kind of assessment by listing both "prouds" and "sorries" when looking at recent performance.

* A fifth source of data is the policies and goals set by those above us in our systems. These must be related to as we set our own goals. The division of student affairs needs to coordinate its goals with the institution at large, while the institution needs to reflect the goals of trustees or the system, if it is part of one.

* A sixth source of information is the thinking of industry experts who are studying future trends in higher education. These experts can provide perspectives that expand our thinking in areas like student demographics, technology, teaching and learning, and education finance.

* A seventh source of input to help us think creatively is a scan of the goals and successes of peer institutions or others whose situation is relevant to ours. It is important, however, to beware of thinking that a practice that has worked somewhere else will work at our own institution. It is more useful to think about what others are doing as offering possibilities that will spark innovative thinking.

* The final source will come from the team itself by mapping the events, trends, and developments (ETDs) that the organization needs to keep in mind as it thinks about the future.

Examples of Forces, Trends, and Developments Affecting Strategy in Higher Education

Four of the most important factors affecting strategy in institutions of higher education are changes in resources, demographics, technology, and the market environment.

Shrinking resources. As public support for colleges and universities has declined over the past 25 years, tuition and fees have been rising at 2-year and 4-year institutions. Between 2000–2001 and 2010–2011, prices for undergraduate tuition, room, and board rose 42% at public institutions and 31% at private not-for-profit institutions (National Center for Education Statistics, 2012). One result has been a student loan debt crisis. Another has been efforts to increase revenue and cut costs that have included increased use of low-cost adjunct instructors, staff reductions, and wage freezes as well as stepped-up marketing and recruitment of new students. Somehow, the vision will need to include ways to make resources more productive in a way that is sustainable.

Changing demographics. Demographic projections are driving change on college campuses. The number of high school graduates is projected to drop sharply. Colleges must go farther afield for a sufficient number of applicants, including internationally. High school populations are becoming more diverse, and more prospective applicants are low-income and first-generation students. Perhaps the most troubling shift in demographics is the large number of students who come to college underprepared. Only about a quarter of high school graduates who took the ACT in 2013 met all four of its college-readiness benchmarks, in English, reading, mathematics, and science (Breuder, 2014). Only 9% of students whose parents did not go to college met all four benchmarks. The implications for what services these students will need are formidable.

Technology. Technology's impact is felt in several ways. Technology is changing how and where teaching and learning take place. It is changing how student services are delivered. The work of a division of student affairs is heavily influenced by technological innovation. Transactions like applying for student aid, registering, and even academic advising are likely to take place online without any face-to-face contact. The student affairs function now has the capacity to use data to track students with computer-based early warning systems. Technology is changing how students are recruited and admitted. Data mining to identify and target the most desirable students is common in a competitive education marketplace.

Political and market accountability. There is an increasing emphasis on accountability for higher education. Governments at the state and federal levels are measuring retention rates, graduation rates, job placement rates, and a host of other metrics. Nonprofit organizations such as the Gates Foundation, the Lumina Foundation, and Complete College America are pushing a social agenda of increasing the percentage of Americans that have post–high school credentials of some kind. The business sector is pushing for employees who are ready to step into a workplace that is becoming more virtual and volatile every day.

EXAMPLE OF THE WORKFLOW FROM FUTURING TO PLANNING

Consider how this process might work using a division of student affairs as the system. The flow of processes is comparable, with some variations, to what might happen in a college, a department, or in the institution as a whole. This workflow has been described in various iterations by Smith, Lippitt, Noel, and Sprandel (1981) and Lippitt (1982).

1. **Select participants for a futuring session.** The CSAO invites key people in the division to participate in a 3-hour session to explore the model of futuring and planning. The group is led by the CSAO and includes all direct reports (e.g., registration, housing, financial aid, advising, student life, security, etc.) as well as those from the second and third levels to represent the horizontal and vertical structure of the division. Individuals are chosen on the basis of age, sex, and race, as well as location within the system and evidence of leadership, initiative, and respect. Representatives from other parts of the university whose voices are important are also invited (e.g., institutional research, finance, marketing).

    Individuals are chosen on the basis of age, sex, and race, as well as location within the system and evidence of leadership, initiative, and respect.

2. **Gather data.** The session begins with participants seated at small tables of five to eight people. Each table represents

a microcosm of the entire group, with a good mixture of levels, roles, demographics, and experience. Several activities (e.g., review of university strategy; history wall; environmental scan of forces, trends, and developments) could be used to build the common database of information at the individual tables and then shared with the entire room.

3. **Preferred futuring.** The participants, still in small, heterogeneous table groups, are told to imagine that they can travel ahead in time to see the campus 5 years into the future. They are asked to observe evidence that the division has transformed itself into an exciting, innovative, and highly effective force having a tremendous impact on student success. Together they use brainstorm callouts to create a vivid and concrete set of dozens of images that are part of their desired future. The work of the tables is posted on the walls and everyone has 10 votes to cast for their top-priority images.

4. **Scenario building.** A working group of leaders is formed to review all of the prioritized future images and look for themes that can be combined into a concrete scenario that describes in some detail what the desired picture of possibility might look like. During this process, members of the group bring everything they know individually to the process, including an assessment of what might help or hinder achieving the emerging vision.

5. **Decisions on strategic goal priorities.** Based on the draft vision, the team considers the gap between the present

state and the desired future state and develops recommendations for goal statements that focus organizational efforts. This draft is reviewed and approved by the senior leadership team.

There are many possible variations on this process and who might be involved. The principles of moving through the strategic planning model, as guided by the leader, do not change. This process of vision creation has two simultaneous benefits. First, senior leaders are more ready to lead the coming change. They have learned together, imagined together, and become aligned around a vision that can then be taken as a draft to the rest of the organization. They have a much more holistic view of the organization as a system and know that their individual voices have been heard. Second, the process has combined the best thinking of a diverse set of individuals so that the resulting vision reflects multiple factors that could not be seen by any single individual or small group.

Having a vision, no matter how compelling, is insufficient by itself to bring about systemic transformational change. If we think of change as a process, the next job of the CSAO is to design the architecture of the journey.

REFERENCES

Breuder, D. R. (2014, January 17). Generating first-generation students. *The Huffington Post*. Retrieved from http://www.huffingtonpost.com/dr-robert-l-breuder/generating-firstgeneratio_b_4611814.html

Dannemiller Tyson Associates. (2000). *Whole-scale change: Unleashing the magic in organizations*. Ann Arbor, MI: Berrett-Koehler.

Lippitt, R. (1982). *Future before you plan.* Retrieved from http://www.moregrads.com/wp-content/uploads/2014/10/Future-Before-Plan.pdf

National Center for Education Statistics. (2012). Tuition costs of colleges and universities. Retrieved from https://nces.ed.gov/fastfacts/display.asp?id=76

Smith, L. N., Lippitt, R., Noel, L., & Sprandel, D. (1981). Mobilizing the campus for retention: An innovative quality of life model. Iowa City, IA: The ACT National Center for the Advancement of Educational Practices.

CHAPTER 7

The CSAO as Change Architect

Albert B. Blixt and Laurence N. Smith

There is a saying that every building is built twice: once in the mind of the architect and once by the hand of the artisan. So, too, is the vision of the preferred future, if it is to become a reality. The architect's plan for a new house will not only show where the walls and windows will be, but will also take account of how it will be built and who will build it. The chief student affairs officer (CSAO) must lead the change process to specify both what needs to be different in the organization and how people will be engaged to make those changes. The CSAO needs a framework to guide that dual process.

THE STAR OF SUCCESS IS THE ARCHITECT'S GUIDE

A division of student affairs is a system with many moving parts. On a larger scale, the same is true for a college or university. Each of the components of the system interacts with others. If you change one thing to fix a problem, it will have unintended consequences somewhere else. The only way to have successful change

> *If you change one thing to fix a problem, it will have unintended consequences somewhere else.*

is to recognize and account for the complex nature of these interactions. The Star of Success Model[1] (Dannemiller Tyson Associates, 2000), illustrated in Figure 7.1, shows the interaction among five key aspects of successful organizations. These are (1) strategic direction, (2) function, (3) form, (4) resources, and (5) shared information. Designing the change process needed to implement the strategy and achieve the vision requires awareness of how the various factors work together.

---

[1] The Star of Success Model was developed by Allan Gates, Albert Blixt, Kathleen Dannemiller, Paul Tolchinsky, Sylvia James, and Roland Loup of Dannemiller Tyson Associates.

Figure 7.1. *The Star of Success Model*

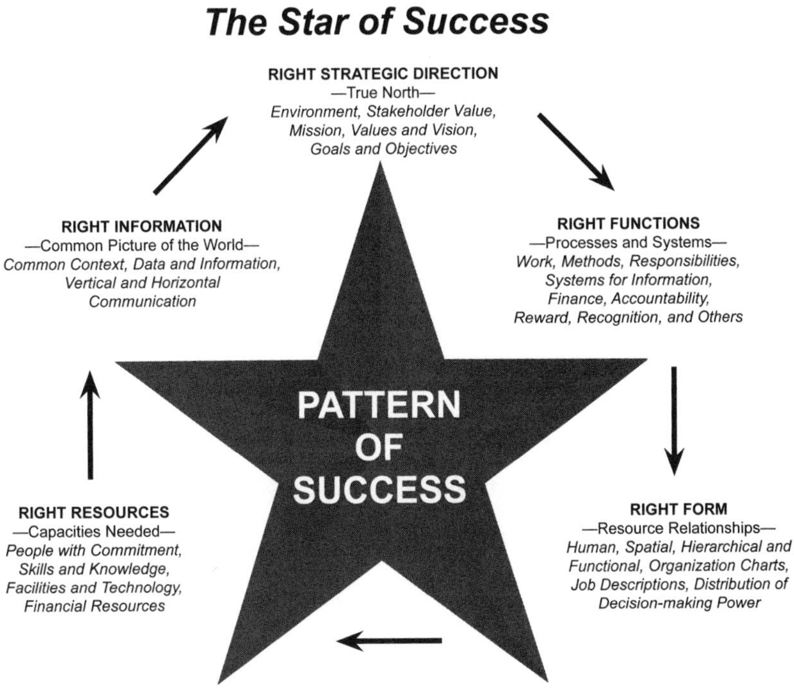

The Star of Success

RIGHT STRATEGIC DIRECTION
—True North—
Environment, Stakeholder Value,
Mission, Values and Vision,
Goals and Objectives

RIGHT INFORMATION
—Common Picture of the World—
Common Context, Data and Information,
Vertical and Horizontal
Communication

RIGHT FUNCTIONS
—Processes and Systems—
Work, Methods, Responsibilities,
Systems for Information,
Finance, Accountability,
Reward, Recognition, and Others

PATTERN OF SUCCESS

RIGHT RESOURCES
—Capacities Needed—
People with Commitment,
Skills and Knowledge,
Facilities and Technology,
Financial Resources

RIGHT FORM
—Resource Relationships—
Human, Spatial, Hierarchical and
Functional, Organization Charts,
Job Descriptions, Distribution of
Decision-making Power

Note. Adapted from Dannemiller Tyson Associates, 2000, p. 222. Reprinted with permission.

Strategic direction. Strategy is the "North Star" of change. It tells the purpose of the organization and where it is headed. The vision, goals, and objectives guide everyone in their daily work. Clear strategic direction coupled with a commitment to continuous learning ensures that course corrections will be made as needed.

Work functions. The road to success is traveled in our daily work. Work processes and systems should be designed for efficiency and effectiveness. In student affairs, core processes might include admissions, registration, academic advising, housing, and financial aid. Support systems needed to enable these core processes include human resources, marketing, finance, training, and information technology (IT). For each aspect of the vision, what are the mission-critical processes and systems? Which are missing or broken? How can we improve them?

Organizational form. Success requires that form should follow function. Getting form right requires designing relationships, roles, and responsibilities in a way that ensures optimal organizational functioning. Form is about how power and responsibility are distributed. It is about how boundaries are drawn. Are roles and responsibilities well defined? Are relationships and the distribution of decision-making power working well? What can we do to make form follow function more effectively? Note that both formal and informal relationships must be considered. Anyone who has underestimated the informal power of an administrative assistant to enable or block one's intentions will understand this reality. Also, external relationships with other parts of the institution and entities outside the institution must be structured to support the work of the organization as much as possible.

> *Form is about how power and responsibility are distributed. It is about how boundaries are drawn.*

Resources. The most well-designed organization will not work without proper resources. People are the CSAO's most important asset. Resource allocation begins with having the right people with the right skills in the right roles who are committed to the vision.

Talent management and development are therefore critical aspects of having the right resources. Achieving the mission also requires the effective allocation of physical, technological, and financial resources. We need to ask whether we have created the conditions best suited to getting the work done. If we want to foster innovation and change, we need to pay special attention to how knowledge management and information sharing are supported. Do we have the right technology? Physical space can be a tremendous resource if we make it easy for people to collaborate by putting them in close proximity and providing the right technology to develop new ideas.

> *If we want to foster innovation and change, we need to pay special attention to how knowledge management and information sharing are supported.*

Information. Good decisions—in both the short and long term—must be guided by information. Channels of communication are both formal and informal. Decision-support information must be accurate, timely, and relevant to the work at hand. We need to ask if we are measuring the right things. Is the information we gather being stored, analyzed, and made available to the people who need it? Do people have enough information to see the big picture, and the right information to make good decisions in their daily work? Creating opportunities for people to talk to each other is just as important as having good IT systems.

Note that the Star of Success Model can be used both to design the system and to evaluate its operation. The Star is a helpful model for looking at the vision for the institution, student affairs, or a particular program within student affairs. Also note that the leader will not have all the answers to these questions. The people in the organization must be empowered to answer those questions and shape the changes that are needed. At a minimum, the CSAOs must educate their leadership teams in the system principles of the Star as they plan and assess.

Assuming there is one "right" answer ignores the power of letting diverse views collaborate, and disempowers employees.

The Change Journey Is a Process

The Whole-Scale Change methodology describes the change process as consisting of a series of events that typically alternate between small and large group interactions.[2] The large group meetings function to enhance understanding, information sharing, and alignment. Small group activities are used to gather data or implement agreed-on actions. This series of alternating steps enables the organization to simultaneously create and implement actions that will lead to the desired transformational change.

The process follows the action-learning approach based on the Action Research Model created by organizational development

---

[2] The Whole-Scale Change methodology was pioneered by the partners of Dannemiller Tyson Associates beginning in the mid-1980s; it has continued to evolve to the present. It consists of a system of theories, models, and processes used to bring about whole-system change.

pioneer Kurt Lewin (1997). The Converge/Diverge Model (Dannemiller Tyson Associates, 2000; Lawrence & Lorsch, 1986) shows how an organization diverges to gather data or implement actions and converges to become whole in order to share and integrate information and make collective decisions about further action. Alternating differentiation and integration encourages small group freedom of action in the context of a common purpose.

One of the benefits of this approach is that it uncovers and combines wisdom with knowledge that exists in the organization but is otherwise unavailable. Many organizations base their change or improvement efforts on the assumptions of problem solving. In fact, assuming there is one "right" answer ignores the power of letting diverse views collaborate, and disempowers employees who might otherwise contribute to innovative solutions. If there is a "right" solution, it follows that other solutions are "wrong." The right/wrong paradigm is limiting and an ineffective way to help organizations change.

> *When those people go back to their local work group, they carry that expanded perspective with them.*

The Converge/Diverge Model, shown in Figure 7.2, illustrates the basic form of the change journey. It represents a flow that integrates the individual, small groups, and the whole system to expand system knowledge (diverge), combine multiple perspectives (converge), test possibilities (diverge), and make systematic decisions (converge). The large ovals in the model depict opportunities for a critical mass of the system to "get whole" (converge). In the flow of convergence and divergence, large group events accelerate the change by uniting people around new knowledge gained from individual and small group experiences. Bringing together people from different levels and functions expands the thinking of the group. When those people go back to their local work group, they carry that expanded perspective with them. In this way, a microcosm group can carry the message of change back into the organization. In the larger group, people can also make decisions that will speed the process and allow people to take "local" action.

Figure 7.2. *Converge/Diverge Model*

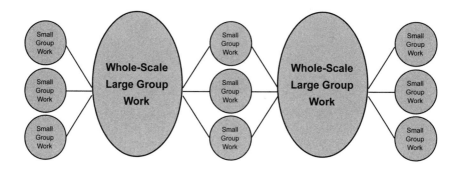

Note. Adapted from Dannemiller Tyson Associates, 2000, p. 11. Reprinted with permission.

THE ARCHITECTURE OF THE CHANGE JOURNEY: AN EXAMPLE OF THE WORKFLOW OF A CONVERGE/DIVERGE CHANGE PROCESS

The Converge/Diverge Model can be used to design a roadmap for any kind of change initiative. Figure 7.3 is an example of a yearlong major change initiative at the university level. The boxes in grey represent whole-system convergence while the remaining boxes represent various kinds of divergence (small group work). In a real-life application, this kind of map would be presented to the people in the organization at some point as a draft. Milestones and timetables can change based on what is actually happening. The idea of a regularly adjusted change roadmap requires that the CSAO and the leadership team monitor and support the effort and communicate regularly with the people doing the work.

Note that the change effort begins with a relatively small group of senior leaders who establish the basic path toward change. In the division of student affairs, this senior team would include directors who report to the CSAO. After that, the circle of involvement is continually expanded, beginning with an extended leadership team that will include persons who are one or two levels below the leader (e.g., managers, supervisors, etc.) and who bring a different perspective. At each step, the draft plan is reviewed and input received. Ultimately, involvement extends to either the whole system (the division) or a significant microcosm of the system. Other support teams may be identified to provide logistical, research, or other support.

Each meeting has a well-defined purpose statement with desired meeting outcomes. Each follows the DVF Formula (described in Chapter 5) in its design—first creating shared information and then agreement on what needs to be accomplished. Finally, participants agree on what next steps are needed. This process of moving from large to small and back again allows for simultaneous learning and action that lets people see the big picture while acting "locally."

Figure 7.3. *Example of a University Change Implementation Process Flow*

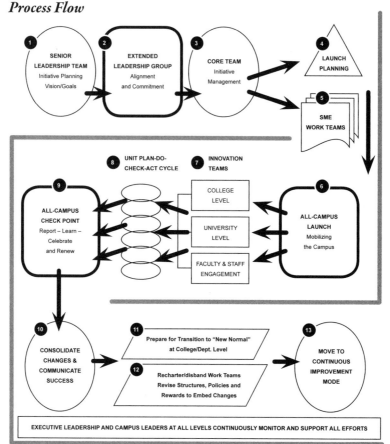

1. Senior Leadership Team meets to plan the initiative, create draft vision of success and set goals.

2. Extended Leadership Group (second- and third-level managers) meets to provide input to the Vision and the implementation plan.

3. A Core Team is formed to provide administrative support to the project. This group will convene and monitor task teams that are needed from time to time.

4. Planning for the All-campus Launch is done by an Event Planning Team made up of a representative sample of leaders, faculty, staff and students who will be part of the All-campus Launch.

5. Subject Matter Expert (SME) Work Teams are formed to work on research and planning for the subject matter of the initiative to make sure information is ready for the All-campus Launch and following activities.

6. All-campus Launch is where a significant microcosm of the campus is engaged. The design of this meeting follows the DVF Formula moving from information to vision of success to next steps action.

7. Innovation Teams are formed at unit and system level to develop ideas and action plans for each level. These teams coordinate with the leadership and with the Core Team.

8. Plan-Do-Check-Act Cycle has people in their functional work groups taking action to work toward strategic objectives guided by the vision of success.

9. All-campus Check Point is held at 6 or 12 months to bring everyone back together to assess progress, celebrate success, and plan further steps.

10. Consolidate Changes means lessons learned are being applied and people are settling into new ways of working.

11. Prepare for Transition means integrating the change work into standard operating procedure.

12. Work Teams are disbanded and their functions are either no longer needed or transferred to permanent structures to embed changes.

13. Move to Continuous Improvement as the change shifts from transformation to improvement.

We have seen how the CSAO must assume the roles of visionary and change architect. Next we will consider what the CSAO must do to mobilize people in order to make the change plan a reality.

REFERENCES

Dannemiller Tyson Associates. (2000). *Whole-scale change: Unleashing the magic in organizations.* Ann Arbor, MI: Berrett-Koehler.

Lawrence, P. R., & Lorsch, J. W. (1986). *Organization and environment: Managing differentiation and integration* (rev. ed.). Cambridge, MA: Harvard Business Review Press.

Lewin, K. (1997). *Resolving social conflicts and field theory in social science.* Washington, DC: American Psychological Association.

CHAPTER 8

The CSAO as Change Champion

Albert B. Blixt and Laurence N. Smith

In Chapters 5, 6, and 7 we learned about the theory of change as well as two roles of the chief student affairs officer (CSAO): visionary and change architect. Now we will consider what it takes to actually champion a strategic and transformational change effort. This is the CSAO's role in engaging and managing people to lead them through the change process. To be successful as a change leader, the CSAO must develop specific skills and abilities. From years of experience, we, the authors, have learned that leaders benefit from embracing the following advice.

Be visible. As the leader of the change, you need to make it clear that the vision is your priority. You will need to communicate your passion and commitment continuously. Get out of your office and talk to people. Let them hear from you that this is not some "flavor of the month" that will be soon forgotten. Leadership is not something you can delegate.

Build teams. This change effort will require different kinds of teams. First, you need a strong leadership team to help you manage the change process. This group must take collective responsibility for the work, a new role for many of them who are used to staying in their functional silos. You will also need support teams to handle the administrative tasks of planning meetings, creating communication channels, providing training, and measuring results. Some of these teams will exist only for a short time whereas others will be merged into the permanent organizational structure. Wherever possible, make use of existing committees, teams, and roles rather than inventing new ones. Make a point to see that teams have charters and that there is an established process to measure and reward accomplishments.

> *Leadership is not something you can delegate.*

Create connections. You have an important responsibility to communicate with people, but it is just as important that they communicate with each other. Create opportunities, both formal and informal, for people from across the organization to share what they are seeing, plan together, and celebrate success together. This might mean an occasional town hall meeting, a special Web page that people can post to, or some other mechanism to let people see that change is happening and how they can contribute to it.

Set boundaries and expectations. There are boundaries in the change effort and you need to make them clear. Make sure you have defined roles and responsibilities in ways that encourage collaboration and not conflict or competition. Let people know what authority they have to make decisions and spend

> *Make a point to see that teams have charters and that there is an established process to measure and reward accomplishments.*

money. Also make clear what is expected of each person, team, and functional area. One way to do that is to make change goals part of performance evaluation. Another is to embed roles, responsibilities, and expectations into team charters.

Support innovation and risk taking. You won't get breakthrough change if people are afraid to take chances. Make it clear that you will support intelligent risk taking but that your support is not a license for recklessness. Discuss with your people what kinds of risks are okay and how to prepare for and learn from failure. Everyone should have thought about alternatives, risks, and rewards of any action and have a "Plan B" to fall back on. Sharing stories of courage in risk taking is important. When bad news comes, don't shoot the messenger.

Expect setbacks. There will inevitably be delays and false starts. Teams will be late getting started because they can't find time to meet. Some crisis or another will get in the way. You will discover that people need more training, direction, or time to accomplish things than had been planned. Getting off track is not the problem; the problem is not being ready to get things back on track.

Celebrate success. What excites and motivates people is seeing that change is working. You will need to create ways for people to experience both early and later successes, even if they are small ones. Recognize individuals and teams that are doing a great job. Create opportunities for people to take credit for their innovations. Praise the work of everyone who contributes. A personal "thank you" note from the leader can mean a lot to someone on the front line. It is also important to remind everyone of how far the organization has come as the weeks and months go by. It is all too easy for your staff to be so caught up in the day-to-day work that they simply do not notice that things are better and that they are better because of this change initiative.

> *Getting off track is not the problem; the problem is not being ready to get things back on track.*

Stay the course. Leading and managing change is a race that never ends. Know that your primary role from now on is to keep people focused on the challenge of creating the future. Don't let the distractions of day-to-day crises, institutional politics, or your own need to retreat to your comfort zone keep you down for long. Your long-term success and the success of your organization demand that you demonstrate the willingness and ability to be a visible, passionate, and courageous leader, even on days when you don't feel like it. The rewards will be enormous.

THE CSAO's 8-STEP PROCESS FOR LEADING AND MANAGING CHANGE

Most major change efforts in organizations fail (Kotter, 1995). Why? Because organizations often do not take the holistic approach required to see the change through. They address symptoms rather than root causes. They underestimate the difficulty of getting people to understand and support the change. Over the past 30 years, there has been much research on how to create successful change efforts. Business and academic gurus such as Peter Drucker (2006), D. Edwards Deming (Deming & Orsini, 2012), and John Kotter (1995) have given us insights into the dynamics of change. Organizational development pioneers like Ron Lippitt (Smith, Lippitt, Noel, & Sprandel, 1981; Lippitt, 1982) and Kathie Dannemiller (Dannemiller & Jacobs, 1992; Dannemiller Tysons Associates, 1994, 2000) have provided robust processes for engaging the people in organizations.

> *Don't let the distractions of day-to-day crises, institutional politics, or your own need to retreat to your comfort zone keep you down for long.*

The 8-Step Process listed here, based on Kotter's (1995) model and the work of Lippitt (1982) and Dannemiller Tyson Associates (2000), provides a strategic framework for a change effort. By following these steps, an institution can avoid failure and become skilled at change. By improving the institution's ability to adapt continuously, an institution can increase its chances of success in the near and long term.

Step 1: Create a Sense of Urgency

People don't change unless they are motivated to do so. Organizations have a kind of inertia that keeps them moving in the same direction unless there is a force to cause that direction to change. Colleges and universities are particularly resistant to doing things differently. Your first step as a leader is to build the case for change. People need to see both the risks and the opportunities presented by what is going on inside and outside the institution. If student persistence is a major priority, you will need facts about enrollment that go beyond the standard top-line numbers for retention. If your 6-year graduation rate is 40% (not uncommon) you need to lay out the consequences of not graduating 6 out of 10 entering students. What is the cost in human terms of a student dropping out without a degree but with a mountain of student debt? What new accountability measures are being imposed by state and federal authorities? What does that figure mean in terms of lost revenue to the school? What are the long-term implications for faculty, staff, employers, donors, and prospective students? One of our clients summed up the need for urgency by saying, "If you are not scared by the current situation, you just don't have enough information!"

> *Organizations have a kind of inertia that keeps them moving in the same direction unless there is a force to cause that direction to change.*

Step 2: Build a Leadership Team to Guide the Change

If you are the change leader, you will need to assemble a group with enough power to lead and manage the change effort. You will need to help the group to work as a team. If you are not the leader but a member of the leadership team, you will need to understand your role and how you can support the team. In either case, change is a team sport that requires working across organi-

> *Change is a team sport that requires working across organizational boundaries.*

zational boundaries. So, for instance, if you want to implement a new early alert system, you will need to engage all the necessary functions to participate in that system, including the faculty, academic advisors, information technology, and residence hall staff. Often these are groups that do not have a good track record of working together. Your leadership team can help make the right connections and bring knowledge, resources, and influence to your project.

Step 3: Create a Compelling Vision of the Future

Most institutional vision statements are just bumper stickers that say in a few words what the school wants to be known for. As discussed in the last section, the kind of vision we propose is much more robust than that. Imagining the future in detail is about describing our dreams for the institution. If you can't picture what you want, you can't achieve it. A preferred future statement will be much more multifaceted than a simple phrase or slogan. So if we say we want to have an institution that in 5 years is thriving, that's a beginning. If we say we want our institution to be able to attract, retain, and graduate well-prepared and highly motivated students who are ready to take the next step in their lives, that adds to the picture. If we are able to describe what we want people inside and outside the institution to be thinking, saying, and doing differently in 3 to 5 years, we start to bring that picture into sharper focus.

The process of creating a robust and energizing picture of the future requires engaging the people who are needed to help create it. Leaders have a point of view about the future and they should. Enriching that point of view by getting input from others makes it better and more likely to be supported. It is through uncovering and combining our aspirations that we can harness the potential of the organization.

Step 4: Engage People in Creating the Change

Make sure as many people as possible understand and accept the vision and the strategy. The engagement process goes well beyond simply calling a meeting and lecturing about the change. The people in the organization have a great deal of knowledge about what is and isn't working that leaders simply do not possess. The people in the organization are also a rich source of creativity and innovation. Creating teams and task forces, holding interactive town hall-style meetings, and letting people have a voice in the change

Creating teams and task forces, holding interactive town hall-style meetings, and letting people have a voice in the change effort may feel risky.

effort may feel risky. Our experience is that the more people are trusted and involved, the more likely the change is to be successful.

Step 5: Empower Broad-based Action

Remove obstacles to change. Alter systems or structures that seriously undermine the vision. Encourage risk taking and nontraditional ideas, activities, and actions. Before you can set out on the journey to the future of your dreams, you must first know where you are now. Systemic change is really about three things: *processes, people,* and *information.* Processes describe the work we do and how we do it. People are the ones who do the work, so we need to understand what roles they play, how they are organized, and how they interact. Information is the fuel that drives the organization. We need to understand what information people need to view the big picture and to make wise decisions in their daily work. This largely has to do with what information is gathered (what is measured) and how it is distributed, as noted in the Star of Success Model in Chapter 7. Organizational structures and organizational culture strongly influence how well these three components function in getting to the preferred future.

> *Systemic change is really about three things: processes, people, and information.*

Step 6: Achieve and Celebrate Short-term Wins

Nothing builds momentum for change like achieving victories, even when they are small. Plan for achievements that can easily be made visible, follow through with those achievements, and recognize and reward employees who were involved. When you begin the change effort, look for things that can be accomplished in the first 30, 60, or 90 days. Bring people back together periodically to hear what others have been doing and what can be learned from those efforts. Renew enthusiasm by being highly visible in supporting the change.

Step 7: Be Persistent in Sustaining the Change

Use increased credibility to change systems, structures, and policies that don't fit the vision; hire, promote, and develop employees who can implement the vision; and, finally, reinvigorate the process with new projects, themes, and change agents. Some things will take time. Often change efforts are limited in their first year because the budget is already fixed. Getting the right people into the right positions can be complicated and may take time. Make sure that people know you are in this for the long term.

> *Culture is a pattern of beliefs, attitudes, norms, values, and behaviors that do not change overnight.*

Step 8: Embed the Changes Into the Culture

Culture can be simply defined as "the way we do things around here." Culture is a pattern of beliefs, attitudes, norms, values, and behaviors that do not change overnight. Articulate the connections between the new behaviors and organizational success, and develop the means to ensure leadership development and succession. This means phasing out temporary structures (e.g., pilot programs, task forces, change teams) and integrating the new functions and processes into existing permanent roles. Hire and train new people based on their ability and willingness to support the new culture. Above all, make support of the vision one of the criteria for evaluating individual and group performance at every level.

CONCLUSION

Change is a journey that the leader must be ready to devote time and attention to over time. These eight steps help to frame the beginning, middle, and end of a particular change process. Embedding the change into the fabric of the organization is a major accomplishment deserving celebration. Making the change part of the culture allows the organization to refine and improve its new operating mode. Eventually, circumstances will, sooner or later, require another cycle of renewal as the organization adapts. It is the leader's responsibility to make sure that the lessons of successful change are learned so they can be repeated.

REFERENCES

Dannemiller, K. D., & Jacobs, R. W. (1992). Changing the way organizations change: A revolution of common sense. *Journal of Applied Behavioral Sciences, 28*(4), 480–498.

Dannemiller Tyson Associates. (1994). *Real time strategic change: A consultant guide to large-scale meetings.* Ann Arbor, MI: Author.

Dannemiller Tyson Associates. (2000). *Whole-scale change: Unleashing the magic in organizations.* Ann Arbor, MI: Berrett-Koehler.

Deming, W. E., & Orsini, J. N. (2012). *The essential Deming: Leadership principles from the father of quality.* New York, NY: McGraw-Hill.

Drucker, P. F. (2006). *Classic Drucker: Wisdom from Peter Drucker from the pages of Harvard Business Review.* Boston, MA: Harvard Business Review Press.

Kotter, J. P. (1995). Leading change: Why transformation efforts fail. *Harvard Business Review, 73*(2), 59–67.

Lippitt, R. (1982). *Future before you plan.* Retrieved from http://www. moregrads.com/wp-content/uploads/2014/10/Future-Before-Plan.pdf

Smith, L. N., Lippitt, R., Noel, L., & Sprandel, D. (1981). *Mobilizing the campus for retention: An innovative quality of life model.* Iowa City, IA: American College Testing Program.

CHAPTER 9

Technology and Transformation

Shannon E. Ellis

Higher education is standing at a divide between the familiar, time-honored practices of its past and the challenges of a future filled with disruptive innovation either caused or accelerated by digital technology. This technology affects how information is gathered, analyzed, accessed, and communicated. Digital technology includes hardware, such as computers, smartphones, tablets, closed-circuit television systems, and other devices that have a digital component. It also includes software, programs, websites, and linking devices such as the Internet, Web conferencing, cloud computing, GPS (Global Positioning System) tracking, applications of every description, and data-mining software.

133

The amount of information that can be gathered and made accessible is virtually unlimited. The divide between the world we have known and the world that is coming widens every day. The role of the chief student affairs officer (CSAO) is not only to cross that divide but also to help build the bridges needed so that everyone else gets across safely. While innovation is happening in every sector of the economy, the reality in higher education is rapidly being seen as "innovate or die." That sense of urgency must be considered a driving force for change in student affairs if it is to retain its relevancy.

This chapter describes the impact of technology on the role of the CSAO in leading innovation and change. It explores the transformational role technology must play in the success of student affairs.

> *While innovation is happening in every sector of the economy, the reality in higher education is rapidly being seen as "innovate or die."*

The term "technology" is derived from the Greek and means the study of the use of scientific knowledge for practical purposes. In a broad sense, technology has been with us since the invention of the wheel. The problem is that the nature and pace of technological change has been accelerating for several decades—faster than many of us can adapt to. Visionary computer scientist Alan Kay defined technology as "anything that wasn't around when you were born" (Greelish, 2013, para. 2). In a taped TED conference talk, inventor, scientist, and entrepreneur Danny Hillis (2012) said, "Technology is anything that doesn't quite work yet." These humorous definitions provide a useful context for considering how technology complicates and yet enhances leadership opportunities for the CSAO.

Technology is both a product *and* a process. Products abound. A student affairs budget expends hundreds of thousands of dollars each year on software, such as Target X, Curriculog, and College Scheduler. Hardware, such as smart pens and braille machines, provide accommodations to thousands of students while laptops, tablets, and mobile phones are standard issue to employees. Every day, technological processes afford access and ease for daily work. For example, consider Skype interviews with someone halfway around the world; 24/7 assistance with help lines and Web chat; automatic triggers for scheduled communication flow to prospective students; and academic progress reports sent by faculty with the click of a mouse to students and their advisors.

These concrete examples of the use of technology can obscure the larger systemic implications for the CSAO. Current CSAOs and many of their staff members learned to use technology later in their careers as it evolved. Today's students and younger professionals grew up with this technology. Many CSAOs, when given a choice, are likely to ask students or their children or grandchildren for help with digital devices, raising the question of how prepared these student affairs executives are to make strategic decisions about the role of

> *Current CSAOs and many of their staff members learned to use technology later in their careers as it evolved.*

technology in student affairs. Can they see beyond hardware and software when thinking about the implications of their effectiveness with students of today and tomorrow? Can they look past technology's enabling power to its ability to transform the service, teaching, and development work of student affairs?

All student affairs divisions are in the technology business whether or not they recognize or respond to that fact. Eric Stoller (2012), social media blogger for *Inside Higher Ed* said, "We have institutionalized a laissez-faire attitude towards technology within Student Affairs" (para. 3). An effective CSAO cannot be content to accept a "tech-less" student affairs division. Success in student affairs in the future will be less a matter of what we know than how we use that information. In other words, it's a matter of changing *how we think* in a way that generates more options and solutions. For example, in-person registration was improved with phone registration, which was replaced with an online process that could be accessed from a Wi-Fi hot spot at any time of day or night. Technology stimulates innovative thought and boundary-spanning alternatives. Understanding and applying this same stimulus to student affairs work is the key advantage for an effective CSAO in leading today's transformation economy (Hurson, 2008).

Creating an e-Culture in Student Affairs: New Tools With an Old Purpose

We can define "e-culture" as the conscious application of digital technology in the way that people work and relate to one another. The purpose of creating such a culture is to enable the best qualities of a community. "E-culture derives from basic principles of community: shared identity, sharing knowledge, and mutual contributions" (Moss Kanter, 2001, p. 8). Student affairs professionals and their organizations have a long history of community building as a tool for student engagement, support, and success. The profession will succeed by embracing the culture of community that comes from rapid

> *One of the key attributes of e-culture is that it connects the benefits of technology to those of human interaction.*

technological innovation. As in any community, communication is the heart of e-culture. What is different is that it is faster, more visible, and readily accessible. E-culture fosters a spirit of collaboration as well as emergent strategies and improvisation. It can be fun or it can be threatening, especially when causing dramatic change through disruptive innovation.

One of the key attributes of e-culture is that it connects the benefits of technology to those of human interaction. "High tech high touch" (Naisbett, 1999) is both a principle and a goal that urges student affairs professionals to make the most of technology's benefits while minimizing its detrimental effects. In an age of social media, smartphones, self-service, and 10-second attention spans, "high tech high touch" can enhance student service, teaching, and student development. Examples include massive open online courses (MOOCs), digital textbooks, and videotelephony for counseling sessions and job interviews.

Students want high-tech teachers and service providers, but they also want more face-to-face time and personal connections. The 21st-century buzzword is a "student-centered" campus. This concept reaffirms the enhancement of student relationships (with peers, teachers, advisors, counselors) as a key to student success. It should be pursued with all available resources and skills. In the end, whether or not it is effective or needs to be replaced with other approaches can be determined by just asking students about their experience and how they prefer to receive future information from the school. And it should be noted that "students" includes not only full-time and part-time, residence hall and commuter undergraduate students, but transfer students, post-traditional learners, graduate and professional students, as well as those who are either on campus or online.

Tips for Leading in the New e-Culture of Higher Education

On campuses across the nation, CSAOs are asking how best to use social media, mobile tools, and big data to improve student services, learning, and development. This is evidence of the shift that is transforming student affairs and higher education, by redrawing the boundaries of service and learning and reshaping knowledge sources of value to students. These technological innovations are pressing for change at an ever-faster rate. In an interview with CNN, author Marc Prensky said, "People will always be behind now and that will be a stress they have to cope with" (Joy, 2012, para. 12). There is absolutely no going back. Leading the student affairs organization through digital transformation will require blending new knowledge and capabilities with time-honored leadership competencies and management capabilities.

It is an exciting time to be in student affairs given the rapid evolution of technology and its impact on higher education. Communication channels like social media and mobile devices enable 24/7 connections to students and among students. An effective e-culture organization requires a strong,

This is evidence of the shift that is transforming student affairs and higher education, by redrawing the boundaries of service and learning and reshaping knowledge sources of value to students.

visionary, and innovative leader who is emboldened by technology. That requires the CSAO to develop a clear strategy, streamlined techniques, access to tools, and a willingness to focus investment only in innovations that truly create value for students and the institution. Here are some guiding principles for navigating this unknown future.

Bring Your Pre-technology Experience With You

Cyber space is "full of reinvented wheels" (Moss Kanter, 2001, p. 5). The technology is revolutionary—social media platforms, Google glasses, mobile devices—and the challenges presented are new, but the problems of leadership, organization, innovation, and change are similar to those experienced for many decades. Moss Kanter recommends that leaders not only think differently but lead people in working together in new configurations to take full advantage of the potential of the technology age. This is a challenge to even the most seasoned student affairs professional. The e-culture is full of paradoxes: "The e-world is highly decentralized and hard to control, but it forces organizations to become more integrated—more centralized" (Moss Kanter, 2001, p. 7).

While the e-world can be trendy with fads and gimmicks it is also seriously revolutionary. The issues of leadership and management take on new characteristics yet remain at the core of student affairs work. CSAOs must still use their vast pre-digital experience. This experience serves as a launching pad into a new age characterized by mobility, simplicity, expectations of ease and access, connectedness, sustaining and disruptive innovation, transparency, and improvisation; features, for good or bad, that form the foundation for leading change.

Focus on the Purpose of Your Technology: Connecting With Students

The CSAO who recognizes the transformative power of combining technology for community building with technology for delivering transaction services to students will create a model for others on the campus. Technology can be the tool that allows student affairs leaders to act in generative ways so that practice informs policy instead of the other way around. To create such an environment, the CSAO needs to focus on defining technology in the context of delivering programs, activities, and services to students. Ironically, one of the most difficult aspects of doing so is choosing from a very wide range of options. That choice needs to be based on what makes the most important contribution to student graduation rates. Taking a step back from time to time to see how technology can facilitate the process is a future best practice.

The CSAO's advocacy for sustaining innovation is also important and can serve as a campus model for both innovation and change. Technology that offers engagement (response clickers in workshops), simplicity (digital books), solutions (online counseling), pathways (academic planners), and personalized information (individual portals) can become part of the student affairs

Combining technology for community building with technology for delivering transaction services to students will create a model for others on the campus.

environment and spill over to include others ready to improve their service models. CSAOs need to encourage their staff members to identify innovations in their respective areas that will improve both the quality of the services they offer and how they can be delivered and accessed. Analyzing their utility for the division and synthesizing their application will provide considerable enrichment for both the providers and users. An important caveat is to beware of using technology simply for its own sake, and to resist jumping from one innovation to the next without giving the first a chance.

Understanding the technology is just the first and probably the easiest step. The difficult steps are influencing the organizational culture so everyone is more knowledgeable, aware, and open.

Make Transitions Seamless With Parallel Systems

The successful CSAO will make certain that parallel processes are created to ease the transformation from the present to the future. In addition to being innovative and experimental, a proactive student affairs division organizes the structures and processes necessary to support digital delivery. In reality, this means professionals must be willing to continue to support what's in use while experimenting heavily with emerging options. For example, nearly every student affairs organization that converted from homegrown student information systems to proprietary software such as Banner or PeopleSoft in the past decade kept their old administrative management system up and running, recognizing that development needed to occur over a long period, often spanning multiple years. Fortitude and patience pay off in any change endeavor as new ways of organizing and acting emerge. Adopting new technology is an invitation to learn how to manage change.

> *In reality, this means professionals must be willing to continue to support what's in use while experimenting heavily with emerging options.*

Engage in Creative "Forgetting"

For some, it seems that only the young can master this new, mystical environment. Technology has a history of changing the world. The problem is rarely how to get new, innovative thoughts into your mind, but how to get old ones out. Moss Kanter (2001) suggested giving oneself a "virtual lobotomy" (p. 5)—forgetting everything you know. She recommended approaching the e-world by assuming you know nothing.

Another method of ridding the brain of old thoughts is to understand that uncertainty coexists with rapid technological developments. Want to play a game of uncertainty? Play chess with a 3-year-old, because there are no rules. Day to day we are all playing chess with a 3 year old. Leaders who will be effective in this uncertain future of student affairs will engage in productive thinking, breaking new ground by alternating between creative and critical thinking. The productive thinking dynamic consists of "suspending judgment to generate long lists of ideas and then returning to those lists to make choices by judging the ideas against pre-established criteria" (Hurson, 2008, p. 46).

Adapt Existing Processes by Linking and Simplifying Them

New CSAO thinking also uses the concept of adaptive or assistive technology. This concept commonly refers to devices for people with disabilities that enable them to perform tasks through modifications. In the new way of thinking, the CSAO needs to look for enhancements to a current practice or process so that a problem is solved or a process is made easier. This is often done by linking different processes or simplifying a single complex process. As an example, students, particularly first generation, do not always take advantage of the scholarships available to them simply because they are unaware of the award process. Combining the college admission and scholarship applications reduces paperwork while making sure

New thinking encourages student affairs to design a specific method or solution for a special population for whom an existing process is not working.

all students are given consideration for merit-based aid. New thinking encourages student affairs to design a specific method or solution for a special population for whom an existing process is not working. For example, undocumented students are not eligible for federal aid and typically do not file a FAFSA (Free Application for Federal Student Aid). A campus-based design of an alternative institutional "free financial aid form" allows this population of students on their campus to be reviewed for eligible financial assistance.

TECHNOLOGY'S TRANSFORMATIONAL ROLE

Technology continues to find its way into fundamental institutional practices and processes. No area of the college or university is immune to its impact. Technology has already altered the landscape of what we do, how we do it, and how it helps us remain competitive. What is being confronted are not the sustaining innovations that technology has provided but the disruptive technological innovations that have dramatic force for reshaping how we deliver instruction and services, increase efficiency and effectiveness, create affordability, and preserve values and traditions.

The secret to harnessing technology is to make it *not* technical. Technology is a means to an end, and if that end is something that motivates and inspires, the adoption and application of technology will be embraced. The message needs to be that technology changes people for the better. It helps us achieve our common goals. It helps us serve our mission more effectively. It allows us to make a positive difference in the lives of students and to do that better than ever. Exemplary leaders capture the visionary potential of what

> *Technology is a means to an end.*

technology can offer by making what seems impossible possible. Technology creates new behaviors in students (e.g., making friends through social media channels) and in student affairs professionals (e.g., monitoring social media for unauthorized parties, staying in contact with former students through social media). To be sure, it also poses ethical dilemmas (e.g., drones to spy on a student protest or party) and reshapes time-tested standards (e.g., tracking student use of services through smartphones).

The combination of student affairs technologies and learning technologies can spark innovative educational strategies to address priorities such as access, affordability, and completion. We also should ask what these technologies can do to address issues of substance abuse, hazing, and mental illness? Technology inspires people to think not about what is but about what can be. President Kennedy promised to put a man on the moon by the end of the 1960s while the technology to do so did not yet exist. Technology assures us again and again that problems can and will eventually be solved.

CHANGE READINESS: WHICH COMES FIRST, THE PROBLEM OR THE SOLUTION?

Sometimes the solution comes before the problem and waits for the world to catch up. Sticky notes were invented by accident and no one could think of a good marketable use for them. When a chemical engineer wanted to use adhesive to keep bookmarks in his choir hymnal he suggested that instead of sticking the adhesive to the surface it should be put on a piece of paper that could stick to anything (Bellis, 2014). The rest is history.

> *Steve Jobs noted that "a lot of times people don't know what they want until you show it to them."*

The lesson for leaders in a time of transformational change is to realize that they may be ahead of their times and that unused ideas, skills, and strategies may find a more effective fit in the future. In his 2012 *New York Times* Op-Ed piece titled "Come the Revolution," Thomas Friedman wrote, "Welcome to the college education revolution. Big breakthroughs happen when what is suddenly possible meets what is desperately necessary" (para. 3). Steve Jobs noted that "a lot of times people don't know what they want until you show it to them" (Jones, 2012, p. 127). First, there was the mobile phone, then there were mobile phones with applications capable of sending e-mails, showing movies, taking photographs, facilitating banking, playing games, and more. The world was not clamoring for any of these products. However, consumers found their charms irresistible.

When thinking about technologies that have the potential to be disruptive innovations, the question for CSAOs should be what is the lightbulb, car, airplane, smartphone, or tablet that will be the transformational source for recreating student affairs in the coming decade?

RISK TAKING: THE COURAGE TO FAIL

Fear of failure and playing not to lose are often the best ways to ensure losing in the long run. Technology calls on us to embrace experimentation and learn from failure. It does so in a very public and transparent way that to many is scary. Still, risk taking should be seen not as something to be avoided but as a way forward. Learning what doesn't work has great value in the process of inven-

> *Technology calls on us to embrace experimentation and learn from failure.*

tion through experimentation. Sometimes experimentation gives way to improvisation that truly is making things up as one goes along. The CSAO needs to encourage creative, thoughtful risk taking both of staff and for students. The key is to ask, "Is this risk manageable? What are the unintended consequences (good and bad) that might result? How will we use what we learn if it doesn't work?" In other words, taking risks is not the problem, not planning how to land on your feet is. Unfortunately, this topic is not covered in the education or training most of us receive; it tends to be the result of on-the-job learning. Not every day is going to be better than the previous one, and not every effort is going to be successful or acclaimed. In the long run, however, the prize will not go to those who never experimented or welcomed a new idea and through passive or active aggression tried to keep the new from happening. They will probably disappear along with the enterprise they helped to stifle.

The early days of computer technology were about garage start-ups and ignoring the "big guys" in the industry. The early days were free of policies and regulations, fiscal criteria, and graduate degrees, allowing for flexibility and nimbleness. Technology urges the CSAO and other student affairs professionals to be more free-thinking, to take more risks and generate fewer regulations. We should frequently ask, "If we were starting a student affairs organization from scratch, would it look like the one in existence today? What would we create with a clean slate? What would we never do again?" Technology emboldens people to strike out into new frontiers with curiosity and excitement. It provides the courage to say "yes" more than "no" to students, faculty, and staff. Reclaim the wonder of working with students, changing their lives, and role modeling, and give up perfection for "pretty good."

DIGITAL TECHNOLOGY RESHAPES OUR ORGANIZATIONS

The transformational power of technology is a catalyst the CSAO can employ in both deconstructing and reconstructing the student affairs organization. To do so, the CSAO needs to "flip" the relationship with technology by shifting thinking away from hardware and software toward thought processes and organizational models that add value through access and ease of communication.

We live in a world where we no longer control information. Open lines of communication and the movement of information are disruptive. Students and parents have direct access to the president via e-mail. Twitter followers are instantly aware of the vice president's every move. Facebook alerts students and administrators to underground parties. Cyberstalkers can harass from afar. We can still challenge and support students with technology and, by doing so, reach all students enrolled at the college or university. We can assess outcomes even better with the ana-

Technology is a catalyst the CSAO can employ in both deconstructing and reconstructing the student affairs organization.

lytics we can now collect through technology. We can take attendance in class electronically. Information on student movements through their days can be collected through cell phone turnstiles across campus.

Although the profession may never be ahead of technology, student affairs practices and organizational models will change because of the synergy technology creates. A leader's use of this synergy can be the key to opening up minds, intentionally altering patterns of practice, and breaking down the silos present in all organizations. The multitude of ways to network through technological advances opens the channels for communication and new ways to exchange ideas.

CSAOs should anticipate that future technological innovations will increase accessibility, individuality, transparency, and mobility, and reduce privacy. Examples already include campus surveillance cameras, plagiarism detection software, mobile phone tracking, and big data collection from online classes and website use. CSAOs might soon be asked if drones should be employed for keeping an eye on campus.

TECHNOLOGY'S PROMISE: A NEW, MORE INTERACTIVE CAMPUS COMMUNITY

Organizational patterns of communication will continuously transform and shape the organizational structure and operations of student affairs and the entire campus, leading to the creation of a new kind of campus community. Technology is a team sport. Teams engaged to design student service or development opportunities using technology can be more effective than going it alone. Those teams work best when they include different personal and professional perspectives along with a systems perspective of their work. Kayak.com founder Terry Jones (2012) advised to "hire people who don't fit in" (p. 35). The work may take longer as differences slow consensus, but the synergy created by a variety of ideas will also be stimulated. The CSAO needs to have the skills to integrate these perspectives to achieve better outcomes; opportunities for cross-campus collaboration abound. Technology reminds us that the work of educating students both in and out of the classroom is a campuswide effort. As the Japanese proverb says, "No one of us is as smart as all of us" (Jones, 2012, p. 131). It is often the outlier, not the seasoned veteran professional, who comes to the idea table unshackled and keenly insightful about what the future of the profession can and should be. Imagine what nationwide collaboration within the profession of student affairs could offer in terms of efficiency through an innovative sharing of technology solutions and programs. The notion of a team sport can be extended across institutions and even across states, calling into question current models and distinctions.

FORM FOLLOWS FUNCTION: NEW JOBS AND NEW JOB TITLES

Learner relationship manager, interactive monitor, learning scientist, data scientist, clientologist, and human interaction expert—these new job titles articulate the work of bringing together technology and student success. Technology in student affairs must be laser focused on helping students learn, grow, and succeed.

Perhaps a new role within the profession will be that of "technologer."

Tasks and resources that were once held separate can be transformed by technology. The boundaries between the processes of class registration and monitoring academic progress can be blurred in pursuit of moving students toward graduation. Social sites can transmit everything from messages about financial aid deadlines to responsible use of alcohol. These purpose-driven technologies have the potential to lead to new insights about student engagement, effectiveness, and learning. Perhaps a new role within the profession will be that of "technologer." Like a geographer and anthropologist, this position will interpret student technology use and habits. The data scientist will have the ability to interpret big data that will lead to new and improved decision making related not only to student success but to all campus matters.

Technology presents unprecedented opportunities for networks and coalitions, alliances and partners. As the CSAO pursues the connection between in-class and out-of-class learning and development, technology may have already resolved it. An open learning environment with no "in" and "out of" classroom experience, delivered via free software for an e-learning platform to create online courses with ever changing content (i.e., a Moodle—modular object-oriented dynamic learning environment) or wiki platform rather than a learning management system (e.g., Blackboard) encourages students in new ways and expands the population of learners.

> *Technology presents unprecedented opportunities for networks and coalitions, alliances and partners.*

Knowing what you want and *then* finding the right technology versus the other way around is empowering to a leader. Typically, a media-rich environment, with embedded video and images, presentations, RSS feeds, and so forth gives a student affairs department the greatest latitude for reaching students.

What naturally evolves is a personal learning network connecting students and student affairs professionals to a wide and deep pool of experience in the intersection of education and digital technology. As with learning, the delivery of student services should be as active as possible. All efforts should model dealing with exploration, risk, experimentation, failure, and enthusiasm.

THE CSAO AS TRANSFORMATIVE LEADER: GETTING SERIOUS ABOUT CHANGE

E-culture is a fundamentally different way of pursuing the student affairs mission. Technology can successfully transform student affairs if dramatic changes in organizational thinking and structure also occur. This takes courage, as improvisation replaces strategy and increases dependence on community partners, and jobs change to

Digital density allows for a dynamic use of capacity that wasn't feasible before.

meet the need for ideas, collaborators, evangelists, and thought leaders. In the e-culture, both disruption and conflict must be seen as innovative benefits to be encouraged for the purpose of moving forward.

A transformative leader sees the value of digital density, which comprises big data, social media, and other information technologies that connect billions of people and objects. Digital density allows for a dynamic use of capacity that wasn't feasible before, but taking advantage of this calls for new service delivery models. Big data is a blanket term for any collection of data sets so large and complex that it becomes difficult to process using data management tools and traditional data processing applications. Instead of separate strategies for big data and social media, an innovative leader uses the connections created by digital density (Lopez, 2013, para. 1). Think "mobility" and "cloud computing." For example, Uversity and similar software programs build online communities of incoming freshmen classes.

Creating a culture for change requires giving up perfection in exchange for speed, and learning from one's mistakes. The role of the student affairs leader is most critical in changing values, incentives, expectations, and actions to demonstrate fundamental change. Begin with a common theme and a shared vision and repeat them until their message is internalized. Symbols and signals as well as organizational structure and process must emphasize the change. E-learning and e-service in higher education will provide student affairs staff and champions with the tools they need to cheerlead innovations. Celebrations of success, risk, and failure will be critical early on. It isn't the computers or software that ultimately make the difference, but the fundamental system change that should pervade the student affairs organization and profession.

Student affairs professionals need to get serious about continuous dramatic change, even if it redefines higher education or student affairs as we've come to know them. The good news is that the transformation and change will never end. Student affairs leaders can manage and shape the culture and give it expression. They can set the direction, define the context, and help produce coherence for their organization and the campus at large. Change leaders give meaning to events that otherwise appear random and chaotic. Consider policies that encourage innovation with funds, competitive grants, and celebration of success and failure.

In 1964, Marshall McLuhan prophesied that "the medium is the message" (p. 9). The medium, not the content it conveys, should be the focus of our study because the medium affects society not by the content delivered but by its very characteristics. In this century, technology is the medium *and* the message. It is both transformational and transactional. Its use in learning across the curriculum and outside the classroom in service to students, in conducting research, and in promoting global initiatives is one half of its impact on higher education. The problems it solves, the independence it provides, and the disruption it causes are among the many drivers that make technology a rapid force of change, innovation, and transformation for student affairs. The educational and technological horizon belongs to innovators who are willing to cross boundaries without fear.

> *In this century, technology is the medium and the message.*

The exemplary CSAO professional inspires and motivates innovation: Times of rapid technological change produce upheavals that can be viewed as either threats or opportunities. To stay ahead of change, to anticipate and to create the future, will require a culture with the momentum to seek constant innovation and productive change. (Moss Kanter, 2001, p. 253)

The boundaries of student affairs work and higher education have already expanded well beyond the physical campus. To live with e-culture is to live with change. The student affairs organization must be reshaped for the long-reaching implications of digital developments and the density of digital connections.

REFERENCES

Bellis, M. (2014) *Post it notes*. Retrieved from http://inventors.about.com/od/pstartinventions/a/post_it_note.htm

Friedman, T. (2012, May 15). Come the revolution. *The New York Times*. Retrieved from http://www.nytimes.com/2012/05/16/opinion/friedman-come-the-revolution.html?_r=0

Greelish, D. (2013, April 2). An interview with computing pioneer Alan Kay. *Time*. Retrieved from http://techland.time.com/2013/04/02/an-interview-with-computing-pioneer-alan-kay

Hillis, D. (2012). *Back to the future (of 1994)* [Video file]. Retrieved from http://www.ted.com/talks/danny_hillis_back_to_the_future_of_1994

Hurson, T. (2008). *Think better: An innovator's guide to productive thinking*. New York: McGraw Hill.

Jones, T. (2012). *On innovation*. San Bernardino, CA: Essential Ideas Publishing.

Joy, O. (2012, December 8). *What does it mean to be a digital native?* Retrieved from http://edition.cnn.com/2012/12/04/business/digital-native-prensky

Lopez, J. Z. (2013, October 25). Digital density: Reshaping business models and organizations. *Face It*. Retrieved from http://blog.iese.edu/faceit/2013/digital-density-reshaping-business-models-and-organizations

McLuhan, M. (1964). *Understanding media: The extensions of man*. New York, NY: Mentor.

Moss Kanter, R. (2001). *Evolve! Succeed in the digital culture of tomorrow*. Cambridge, MA: Harvard Business School Press.

Naisbett, J. (1999). *High tech high touch: Technology and our search for meaning.* New York, NY: Broadway.

Stoller, E. (2012, July 18). *Pondering the fallacy of the thread.* Retrieved from http://www.insidehighered.com/blogs/student-affairs-and-technology/pondering-fallacy-thread#sthash.rbWqV4Ud.dpbs

CHAPTER 10

Technology and Rethinking the Student Affairs Service Model

Shannon E. Ellis

Technology has turned the student affairs service model on its head. From a group of separate, loosely coordinated functions, the division needs to become a highly integrated organization where centralized functions are executed through decentralized delivery of programs, activities, and services designed and targeted to meet the special needs of a variety of students. Because of extensive technological advances, the student affairs division has the potential to dramatically improve services to a diverse student body.

New Rules for Moving From a Reactive to a Proactive Service Model

For stakeholders in higher education, "What have you done lately?" is less important than "What do you promise to do next?" This recasting of the student affairs service model will continue to mold the work of the student affairs profession. The CSAO must play a central role in moving from a reactive to a proactive service model. As student affairs professionals, we must anticipate and meet the expectations of a tech-savvy student public. The benchmark now is accelerated processes and the provision of better service marked by high convenience and ease. If schools can already process paperless refunds, automate textbook rentals, tutor students online, and tell students where to find available campus parking spots with a mobile app, then the sky is truly the limit in terms of adding effective and efficient use of technology that can extend to many other areas and operations to provide excellent service.

> *The benchmark now is accelerated processes and the provision of better service marked by high convenience and ease.*

New Rules for Redesigning Student Affairs

Technology enables new models for effective student affairs operations. However, their effectiveness depends on rethinking current procedures and the regulations and rules that enable them.

Electronic signatures, online advising, video interactive mental health counseling, and virtual campus tours are evidence of change. Student affairs can successfully let go of age-old practices governed by rules set in a pre-digital era. But what are the new rules that will accompany these new models for student affairs in higher education?

Rule #1: Monitor and Manage Policies and Processes

Conduct regular policy and process audits to determine which regulations and procedures impede the development and use of student service technologies, while ensuring that new providers meet rigorous quality and service standards. Keep in mind, however, that in these early years of the digital age in higher education, the CSAO must encourage experimentation, which also means occasional failure. Technologies in the service of students hold great promise for ease, access, and engagement. In order to experiment with new technologies and integrate them into service and developmental models, it is important to identify barriers and old ways of thinking and doing, and how to leapfrog beyond them. The goal is to synchronize the policy formation cycle with the student services practice cycle. This requires fortitude to allow for the evolution of system-level change.

> *In these early years of the digital age in higher education, the CSAO must encourage experimentation, which also means occasional failure.*

Rule #2: Master the Tools of Student Engagement

The effective use of social media by student affairs professionals promotes student engagement. Student affairs professionals have an opportunity to model continuous learning. This is not necessarily easy. Social media are in continuous stages of evolution that, as their potential unfolds, will create even more ways for stimulating communication and building community engagement. For all their amazing potential, social media are still developing, occasionally flawed, always evolving, and we are all trying to figure them out together. Stoller (2012) warned that social media are only as good as we make them: "The tools themselves do not build houses nor do they increase student engagement. We do" (para. 1).

Rule #3: Make Everything Interactive

Interactivity is a necessary characteristic of student services. Blogging, personal websites, Facebook, and Uversity (a campus-customized social networking website for incoming students) promote self-expression, activism, and discourse. The CSAO must vigorously support the development of a campus culture in which students are encouraged to bring their own interests and discoveries into the discussion with researchers, faculty, student affairs staff, and even the student's family and friends. It is also important to discourage anonymity and encourage ownership of ideas and opinions.

Technology can be very personal; the transparency of information allows students to better participate in their own educational success. Personalization is an important characteristic of student affairs offerings and the paradox is that it doesn't need to be done by a person but can be effectively delivered by technology. College students of all ages enjoy the ease of access, mobility, and limitless resources available to them. Institutions—and student affairs in particular—need to capitalize on the benefits of technology while meeting expectations. At first glance, having tablets in a campus dining hall that allow diners to look up nutritional information and caloric intake might seem unnecessary. However, by providing this information interactively, rather than posting it on the cafeteria wall or making it available in a brochure upon request, conveys important knowledge that gets attention. There is a greater chance it will result in healthier food choices by students. As tablets now outsell personal computers the message is clear that students, like the rest of consumers, continue to favor mobile devices over PCs. But even the smart-connected device market will become old technology some-

> *The message is clear that students, like the rest of consumers, continue to favor mobile devices over PCs.*

day. Cheaper and ever more portable means of communication will be at our students' fingertips. "Phablets" are already emerging as smartphones and small screens mesh.

Rule #4: Make Student Affairs an Even Better "Student of Students"

A basic adage of the student affairs profession is to be first and foremost "a student of students." Considered "digital natives" (Prensky, 2001), today's traditional-age students represent the first generation to grow up with this new technology as the rest of the population is learning about it as "digital immigrants." The implications of this generational lag are staggering as digital natives come of age and see disparities between what they know is possible and want, and what we are providing. Technology is an extension of our students' bodies and minds, creating a cyborg effect that enhances their abilities. It is important for us to continuously assess the impact of technology on students and how they use it. It is important to integrate that knowledge into the practice of the student affairs profession. Our students have changed radically. We need to keep up with them.

> *The implications of this generational lag are staggering as digital natives come of age.*

The good news is that we have new ways of understanding students and their behavior. Learning technologies allow incremental glimpses into the learning process—glimpses that were unknown a decade ago. Student service technologies do the same. For these technologies to be effective, this information needs to be shared. Institutions acquire large amounts of useful user data from student use of their technology. Campuses collect so much data about students that it becomes hard to manage and apply. CSAOs might follow the corporate model and create a senior-level position similar to what they refer to as a data scientist. Perhaps thinking about how successful Internet companies like Amazon, Facebook, and Google gather data about their customers from their Web use can provide new insights about the design and use of campus websites as well. It is important to note that data on the unfiltered behavior of students using campus technology can convey an honesty that user surveys and straw polls will never achieve.

Keep in mind that today's students are no longer the people the student affairs profession was designed to serve, teach, and develop. Computer games, instant messaging, e-mail, the Internet, and smart phones are integral parts of their lives. It is now clear that as a result today's students think and process information fundamentally differ-

> *Our students have changed radically. We need to keep up with them.*

ently from their predecessors. Prensky's (2001) work on these digital natives indicates that the differences go further and deeper than most educators realize. Thinking patterns have changed, according to Prensky's research. Students are used to receiving information very quickly; they like to parallel process and multitask. They prefer graphics to text. Students prefer random access (hypertext) and function best when networked. They thrive on instant gratification and frequent rewards.

Rule #5: Recognize the Digital Natives Won't Go Back

Digital immigrant student affairs executives should recognize that students are not the same as when they were in school and that the same methods that worked when they were students will not necessarily work for students of today and tomorrow. Should digital natives learn the old ways, or should digital immigrants learn the new? "Unfortunately, no matter how much the digital immigrants may wish it, it is highly unlikely the digital natives will go backwards. It may be impossible and their brains may already be different" (Prensky, 2001, p. 3). Smart student affairs digital immigrants accept that they don't know everything about e-culture, and take advantage of opportunities to learn. So communicate in the language and style of students: faster, less step-by-step, with random access. These students are publicly online and they share knowledge. They tap into the wisdom of the crowd. They believe

> *Digital immigrant student affairs executives should recognize that students are not the same as when they were in school.*

that transparency yields trust. These natives are timely, not time managed. They believe in interactions, not transactions. Retain some of the old content (developing mentor connections), get rid of the less important (e.g., land lines, computer labs), and focus on the future (e.g., wireless access, online processes). That future is digital and includes civility and integrity. The effective CSAO needs to reinvent digital native methodologies for work with students at all levels.

Rule #6: Understand That Today's Students Process Information Differently

Another angle in understanding students is assessing the impact of technology on how students think and process information. Research by Clifford Nass (2010) at Stanford University found that the average college student accesses three media sources simultaneously, and 25% actually use four or more. His research on the social and psychological aspects of human–media interaction indicates that such simultaneous use impedes their ability to focus on relevant information and to *pay attention*. Nass (2010) argued that this inability to process information effectively makes multitaskers less thoughtful and more inclined to exercise poor judgment. His research also indicates that such multitaskers have problems with social interaction. Nass (2010) asserted that the multitasking is rewiring people's brains.

If these inabilities and problems are true, the implications for learning, development, and service are profound. The question before student affairs on today's college campuses is how to prevent potential social and psychological harm in an era when even children possess smartphones. Reviewing the national research, as well as con-

> *The average college student accesses three media sources simultaneously.*

ducting your own on your students, can help when developing programs and services, expectations, and protocols both in and out of the classroom. It might also provide insights on how to best serve new generations of students and even new staff who grew up in an increasingly screen-saturated, multitasking modern world.

WARNINGS ABOUT TECHNOLOGY AND STUDENT AFFAIRS EXECUTIVE LEADERSHIP

There is no question that the CSAO will be navigating uncharted waters in the years to come. In addition to the rules above, consider this cautionary advice.

* Create divisional capacity for dealing with technology. Just as there are student affairs administrative departments for other functions, headed by a director with staff and resources, the future demands creating one that deals with technology, social media, data management, and transactional services.

* Stop wringing your hands over technology—it is here to stay. If Coursera can entice the top universities to put their most intriguing courses online for free to bring the best-quality education to anyone in the world, then student affairs can bring its own disruptive innovations to the profession and to higher education. Student affairs practitioners need to encourage their professional organizations to play an instrumental role in advancing campus capacity for using technology to serve students. In his 1869 inaugural speech, Harvard College President Charles Eliot said we are "obligated to use better tools than the old; to devise or transplant . . . prompter and more comprehensive means than the prevailing, and to command more intelligent labor in order to gather rapidly and ensure the best fruit . . . and have time for other harvests" (Morison, 1930, p. 31). Problem solving, improved delivery, new ideas, and aspirational goals are *exactly* what should be expected from technology. This is an agenda not only for the campus but for the professional organizations as well.

> *Stop wringing your hands over technology—it is here to stay.*

✽ At best, technology supports and improves human life; at worst, it alienates isolates, distorts, and destroys (Naisbett, 1999). The uses and abuses of technology are continuous reminders of its evolutionary process. Technology is evolving just as the profession of student affairs is evolving. In his 2013 book *Higher Education in the Digital Age*, former Princeton University President William Bowen urged a balanced commitment to the continuing importance of teaching, service, and pedagogy in higher education even as he advocated for the solutions brought on by the digital age. His humane views and values are couched in concern and excitement about the new educational technologies.

✽ Student service and learning technology opens the doors to any organization that can help students make their way through higher education, thus creating a new world of student affairs competition. Technology reminds the student affairs profession that it must keep up with the times in order to stay relevant and competitive. Much of what was delivered on paper or in person is now readily accessible and easier to use because of technology. Think about setting forth technological expectations in all staff job descriptions. Push to create new positions with innovative titles that meet the technological needs of students and those who serve them.

✽ All the talk of using technology to save money by increasing productivity has a hollow ring. This can, in fact, be true. This is why an effective leader in the digital age will use his

Explore return-on-investment metrics for student service systems, leveraging the transparency and measurement that embedded technologies make possible.

or her critical thinking skills, advice from trusted sources, and analysis of the facts to determine wise return on investments instead of throwing money at technology. For example, advances in technology suggest that online learning can lead to good learning outcomes and online services can lead to better customer satisfaction. Explore return-on-investment metrics for student service systems, leveraging the transparency and measurement that embedded technologies make possible.

* Be patient. These are early days. It is too much to expect that technology has all the answers. It is possible to identify the key questions and pursue the answers in a multitude of forums both inside and outside the academy. What is needed is patience and persistence, study and discussion, optimism and healthy skepticism in this multidirectional and layered world of educational technology.

The Student Affairs Service Model of Tomorrow

Student affairs executives are fortunate to be leaders in this age of rapid technological development. The opportunities presented by these developments ensure ongoing transformation of the student affairs service model. Technological innovations can greatly enhance our effectiveness in helping students succeed, which remains at the heart of the student affairs service model. Student affairs executives must make the choice to enhance their leadership portfolio with enough knowledge to navigate the field, to hire talented people who also embrace technology, and to constantly refresh the resources allocated to technological offerings. In this way, student affairs program and service delivery will have the positive outcomes we expect for our students. It is even possible the student affairs model can have an even greater impact due to technology.

For too long student affairs has let technology tell the profession what to do. It's time that student affairs professionals tell technology what we expect from *it*. The relationship between technology and student affairs is complicated and emerging. This new relationship with technology will not only harness its capabilities for student access, engagement, information, and communication but also will re-create the curriculum, reform use of campus space, reinvent alumni connections, and provide accountability through transparency. In addition to providing services, development, outreach, and programs, student affairs can wield greater influence outside the organization and throughout the institution.

> *It's time that student affairs professionals tell technology what we expect from it.*

The technology necessary to achieve this has arrived and will continue to vastly expand the capacity of the student affairs profession. Technology will provide the means of transformation while remaining an issue to be addressed on the change agenda. Meet these challenges with a sense of renewed optimism. Lead with the new thinking that is needed on the role of student affairs professionals in the e-culture of higher education. Student affairs has the potential to bring about fundamental change that will make higher education more effective and students more successful. The organizational lines are blurred, jobs are changing, gatekeepers to information and decisions have been usurped by open access, and decision making has been recalibrated. The involvement of student affairs is essential. Leadership by student affairs is imperative. Harnessing technology for transformation and transaction is the future not only of the profession but of higher education as well. Be fearless, be open, and claim the horizon of innovation and change as the domain of student affairs.

REFERENCES

Bowen, W. G. (2013). *Higher education in the digital age.* Princeton, NJ: Princeton University Press.

Morison, S. E. (1930). *Development of Harvard University since the inauguration of President Eliot 1869–1929.* Cambridge, MA: Harvard University Press.

Naisbett, J. (1999). *High tech high touch: Technology and our search for meaning.* New York, NY: Broadway.

Nass, C. (2010). *The man who lied to his laptop: What machines teach us about human relationships.* San Francisco, CA: Current Trade Publishers.

Prensky, M. (2001, October). Digital natives, digital immigrants. *On the Horizon, 9*(5), 1–6.

Stoller, E. (2012, August 5). *Social media increases student engagement.* Retrieved from http://www.insidehighered.com/blogs/student-affairs-and-technology/social-media-increases-student-engagement#sthash.IT8qND06.dpbs

CHAPTER 11

Building Capacity for Innovation and Change— Creating a Learning Culture

Stephen J. Gill

The rate at which an organization learns may be the only sustainable competitive advantage. . . . If you are learning more rapidly than the competition, you can get ahead and stay ahead. (Garvin & Edmondson, 2008)

In a video interview with *Harvard Business Review*, Harvard Business School Professor David Garvin defined organizational learning as containing two elements: (1) the organizational process of creating, acquiring, transferring, and retaining knowledge; and (2) the modification of the organization's behavior to

We might assume that colleges and universities would be good at organizational learning, but they aren't.

respond to that new knowledge (Garvin & Edmuonson, 2008). We might assume that colleges and universities would be good at organizational learning, but they aren't. These "centers of knowledge" know how to teach. Learning is another matter. That's because they haven't learned how to learn as an organization. Unfortunately, it is rare for a university or college, as a whole, to intentionally become smarter about how their institution functions.

Jeffrey Selingo (2013), editor at large for *The Chronicle of Higher Education* and author of *College (Un)Bound,* wrote:

Unlike newspapers and bookstores, colleges are mostly protected from market forces by large government subsidies and a complex regulatory environment that does not allow you or me to simply start a new college from our bedroom like we can a website that puts a newspaper out of business. Although as many as a thousand colleges are at risk of closing or merging in the decade ahead because of poor finances, the vast majority of colleges will adapt. Colleges are like cities. . . . They evolve as needs change, although many of them will struggle through this next evolution. (p. xvi)

Organizational Learning Comes With Levels and Barriers

Organizational learning is a set of processes that takes place at multiple levels: the individual level, the small group (team) level, and the organizational (system) level (Gill, 2000). Individual learning happens when a person develops the knowledge, skills, and motivation to help the organization succeed at achieving its goals. This can happen through training or through knowledge acquired on the job. Individuals must master the knowledge acquisition skills needed for their role and they should be able to apply new information in a way that benefits the whole organization. Individuals need to be curious and willing to go beyond following established procedures.

Small group learning works best when members of the group learn how to contribute to the success of the group as a whole. Such groups may be permanent functional units or temporary task teams that bring together individuals from diverse parts of the organization. In any event, these groups function as high-performing teams to achieve outstanding results by continuously acting, evaluating, and adjusting to create new and more effective solutions. This is an interactive process that works best when group members have mastered both individual learning skills and team participation skills.

Whole-organization learning takes place when the systems and ongoing processes are integrated to optimize the functioning of individuals and teams in service of organizational goals. Such learning implies a culture and work environment that actively supports learning, by addressing potential barriers including the following:

* **Functional isolation/silos.** Student affairs is a collection of professional interests divided into functions and programs such as admissions, registration, housing, advising, counseling, and career services. The division needs to transform itself into integrated groups of thinkers working collectively on solving complex problems. Student affairs professionals have a difficult time breaking through the walls they have created for themselves. This tendency toward separation and isolation prevents information from flowing among the people who need it to make decisions that will lead to student success and, ultimately, organizational success.

> *Student affairs professionals have a difficult time breaking through the walls they have created for themselves.*

* **Lack of rewards for learning.** What gets measured and rewarded is what gets done. Most of our measurement and reward systems are based on individual performance. Some of the most important outcomes are the result of complex interactions that are not the work of one person. Staff members are rewarded for performing their assigned tasks. Faculty are rewarded for doing research, publishing, finding funding, and teaching in very narrow areas of study. Until people are rewarded for connecting their individual

and team performance to the achievement of system goals, those goals will not be the focus of their effort.

* **Lack of a feedback mechanism.** Colleges and universities rarely have a mechanism for helpful feedback from their stakeholders (i.e., faculty, students, staff, community partners). Student feedback focuses on the likability of faculty and, maybe, retention of knowledge. These surveys and tests tell us little about what can be done organizationally to improve learning and success for all students. Institutionwide feedback from faculty and staff is rarely specific enough to apply to improving organizational performance.

* **Traditions that resist change.** Institutions of higher learning are steeped in tradition. Whether it's the ivy-covered halls or the gridiron, identity and loyalty are maintained by consistency. Just try changing the name of the football team or moving the location of commencement and you'll quickly find out how important tradition is to students, alumni, and faculty. Change is not valued. In fact, it is discouraged.

THE CSAO MUST OPEN THE DOOR OF OPPORTUNITY FOR STUDENT AFFAIRS

The chief student affairs officer (CSAO) is perfectly positioned to facilitate organizational learning. Colleges and universities cannot continue to compete on the basis of academic programs, or location, or a reputation earned in a different era.

To be competitive, these institutions have to demonstrate that they can make a difference in students' lives. They have to compete on the basis of the student's total experience. They have to show that students at their institutions enjoy being students, complete programs, acquire competencies, earn certificates and degrees, and get jobs in their chosen careers.

> *Some of the most important skills they need are not learned in the classroom.*

Today's colleges and universities have to prepare students of all ages for a world of work that is continually in flux. Some of the most important skills they need are not learned in the classroom. Students need to learn leadership, teamwork, problem solving, creativity, and innovation. They need to know how to work independently and in networks. They need to become agile in what and when they learn. And, most important, they need to learn how to learn, because they will be lifelong learners.

This takes total system effort. The degree of collaboration throughout the campus will determine the magnitude of the institution's success. The division of student affairs will be most effective if it can become one team focused on its members working together to optimize the learning experience of every student through an integrated, interdisciplinary, intradivisional approach to foster student success. And in the process, the divisional team will continually learn how to be more effective so it can become a disruptive, innovative force in how students are educated.

Who better to facilitate the development of a learning culture than the CSAO and the division of student affairs? (Refer to

Chapter 4 to see how an Innovation Center can become a platform for organizational learning and involving others.) The people of student affairs have a holistic perspective on student needs. They view students from every vantage point—from recruitment, to enrollment, through academic progress, to graduation, to life as alumni. The CSAO is able to bring all the various stakeholders to the table in a nonthreatening way. This puts the CSAO in a unique position to ask questions that cause stakeholders to reflect on and learn from experience. First, however, divisional leaders must help their own staff members discover how to learn as a division so they can contribute to creating a learning culture across the institution. Innovation and change depend on this sharing of knowledge across the institution.

The CSAO can bring stakeholders together and ask the audacious question, "Are we, as an institution, aligned to serve individual student needs and maximize student success?" If the answer is "no" or "not entirely, we can do better," then the CSAO can facilitate conversations about what can be done as a total organization, not separating student affairs from academic affairs and operations. Somebody has to ask the tough questions that facilitate organizational learning. This is a perfect role for student affairs professionals.

THE FIRST PRIORITY OF ORGANIZATIONAL LEARNING: UNDERSTAND YOUR STUDENTS

The evolving demographics of the United States are putting pressure on higher education institutions to become more responsive to a wider spectrum of students. Recent high school graduates—who we usually think of as traditional college students—are now a minor fraction of the total student population. And they arrive on campus with different skills, attitudes, and expectations than those of previous generations. The growing segment of adult learners wants to take courses that will help them move up in their current jobs, start new careers, and live fulfilling lives in retirement. The growing international student segment wants to use U.S. colleges as a way to either integrate into U.S. communities or return to and be successful in their native countries.

Recent high school graduates—who we usually think of as traditional college students—are now a minor fraction of the total student population.

At the same time, large numbers of students are attending college unprepared for their studies. Their reading, writing, and math skills are not college level. Many are working full time in addition to going to school and, therefore, can become overwhelmed. This is especially true for the community college population.

Every college and university has a multitude of data on its students. Unfortunately, those data are not organized or applied to learn what students want and need or how to create the conditions that will make them more successful. From Google and Amazon to your local grocery store, merchants of all sizes keep personal data on customer preferences and behavior. They are able to understand preferences and anticipate behavior in order to enhance the customer's experience. How many higher education institutions know as much about their students? Can we help a student choose a career or a roommate or an internship opportunity based on predictive data? If not, how can we gain that capability?

CREATING A LEARNING CULTURE IN STUDENT AFFAIRS

Colleges and universities must develop a community in which administrators, faculty, and staff are constantly sharing information and seeking performance improvement through new knowledge, new skills, and new applications of knowledge and skills to achieving the goals of the institution. They must examine what they do, compare that to what needs to be done, reflect on what they have learned from their actions, and make the needed changes in the organization. Learning how to do this effectively will have huge, long-term benefits for the institution.

> *Colleges and universities must develop a community in which administrators, faculty, and staff are constantly sharing information and seeking performance improvement.*

The division of student affairs, led by the CSAO, can guide the way; but this will mean creating a learning culture within the division, with a focus on innovation and change. Staff will need to learn how to innovate, to manage change, and to continue learning from what they do and from others. To overcome barriers to a learning culture, the CSAO must create a routine of feedback, reflection, and active social learning.

Signs that a learning culture is thriving include:

* Learning is a performance goal for all staff.

* Clear expectations have been set for staff performance.

* Knowledge management systems are in place to facilitate knowledge sharing.

* Employees have designed a personal learning plan that is part of their performance evaluation.

* Individual and team learning activities are recognized and rewarded.

* Teams are involved in action learning.

* Physical workspace is conducive to learning.

* Individual, team, and organizational outcomes are continually assessed and information is used to modify efforts to optimize impact.

A learning culture's effectiveness depends on a high degree of stakeholder interaction. In order for colleagues to continually connect with one another in meaningful ways, there are a few requisite conditions:

* The environment is one of trust, in which honesty, integrity, and a sense of responsibility are valued and reinforced through communication, training, performance feedback, and program evaluation.

* Risk taking is encouraged as appropriate behavior for inventing new approaches and finding solutions to old and emerging problems. Because even calculated risk taking has the potential to fail, staff need to know that failure

will be seen as a learning opportunity not as a reason for punitive action.

* Communication happens frequently so that information and ideas are shared—top-down, bottom-up, and laterally. This leads to success. A lack of information increases the potential for failure, the need for do-over work, mistrust, and rumors. Maintaining continuous and open communication among all administrators and staff provides the context for successful outcomes.

* Employees are engaged as colleagues and are invited to share their knowledge, experiences, and ideas about issues and challenges confronting the division. This builds ownership and support and reduces resistance to new ideas.

> *Because even calculated risk taking has the potential to fail, staff need to know that failure will be seen as a learning opportunity.*

Beyond these interpersonal processes, the CSAO also needs to deal with the organizational barriers to learning that are inherent in the departmental structure and can be especially difficult when departmental objectives compete with divisional initiatives. Employees are used to giving primacy and loyalty to departmental objectives. CSAOs need to consider new organizational arrangements to provide the structure that will put learning to innovate and change at the forefront. Short-term gains need to be replaced with

> *A solution might be to assign an associate CSAO to implement the Innovation Center.*

long-term viability. A solution might be to assign an associate CSAO to implement the Innovation Center and to share in the accountability for its success. Including support for the Innovation Center and its learning objectives as part of each divisional executive's performance plan and evaluation will also help.

THE ORGANIZATIONAL LEARNING TOOLKIT

Many tools are available to help student affairs professionals develop a learning culture in their organizations (Gill, 2010). The following three methods are especially important.

Action learning. This is intentional learning in the process of doing. This kind of learning includes: reflection-on-action, reflection-in-action, and reflection-for-action (Schon, 1983). In applying action learning, participants take time for reflection. They discuss what happened, how it happened, what went well, what could be improved, and what they plan to do next time to increase the likelihood of success.

Organizational self-assessment. How is the student affairs division performing and what can it do better to serve the needs of students and the institution? These questions could be addressed through a survey, focus groups, interviews with key stakeholders, or any number of other methods. The important thing is to get stakeholders to focus on the data and the implications for how the organization as a whole functions.

Appreciative inquiry. This is a method to make everyone aware of the positive experiences and successes of the division. Briefly stated, appreciative inquiry means finding out what works and doing more of it. It is about finding strengths rather than finding problems. The focus of appreciative inquiry is on what has gone well and what can be learned from those successes. For example, if appreciative inquiry is applied to a leadership development program for college seniors, one might look

> *The important thing is to get stakeholders to focus on the data.*

for stories about the positive impact of a program on students, how students benefit from the program when everything goes right, what happens to students after the program when they begin their careers, and how the program can be improved for future students.

One way for student affairs professionals to think about these tools is to consider the learners and what kinds of tools would help them learn best. Learners fit into four levels: (1) individuals (e.g., students, faculty, staff, administrators), (2) work teams (e.g., departments, task forces, committees, centers, institutes), (3) the enterprise as a whole (i.e., student affairs division), and (4) the larger context in which the CSAO reports (i.e., the institution).

The types of tools that student affairs professionals can use at each of these levels fall into three categories: (1) assessments of level of performance, (2) models of organizational systems, and (3) solutions to overcoming deficiencies. Many assessment tools, such as the A6Q Persistence Analytics and the Community College Survey of Student Engagement, are available for measuring and tracking performance. Organizational system models and improvement solutions are very useful in helping individuals and teams make progress. For instance, staff that need to learn how to work together more effectively in teams might use a model for understanding team functioning and identifying the steps for making team-based decisions. A solution might be writing a team charter. The simple act of creating a team charter can help team members agree on their roles and responsibilities, on the way to learning how to work better together.

> *The simple act of creating a team charter can help team members agree on their roles and responsibilities.*

Implications for Student Affairs Professionals

As long as colleges and universities continue to take a program-by-program approach to change they will never achieve the kind of success that they claim they want. Student retention is an excellent example of this. Like the instruments of an orchestra, the retention players need to listen to each other and play their parts in harmony with what others are doing. What is needed is an institution that systemically supports student success in every corner of the organization, from administration leadership to faculty attitudes to curriculum design to the campus environment. Leave out one component and there is little chance for success.

Leaders must be willing and able to change the collegiate culture in order to support learning. Robert Sternberg (2012) made the following point about the difficulty universities have in going in a new direction:

> Change is not always for the better, of course. But a college or university that is static will inevitably fall behind more dynamic, positively changing institutions. And like any institution that fails to compete, it is on the path to stagnation or death. A dynamic institution will change and, if the change proves to be in the wrong direction, will redirect itself until it finds a sustainable path.... Institutions can change—for the better—if they are able to change, believe they can change, want to change, are willing to appear to change, and have the courage actually to change. (para. 13)

The energy to make this happens begins with a commitment from the CSAO to becoming a learning organization.

REFERENCES

Garvin, D., & Edmondson, A. (2008, December 15). *The importance of learning in organizations* [Video file]. Retrieved from http://www.youtube.com/watch?v=lUP4WcfNyAA

Gill, S. J. (2000). *Organizational learning: The manager's pocket guide.* Amherst, MA: HRD.

Gill, S. J. (2010). *Developing a learning culture in nonprofit organizations.* Thousand Oaks, CA: Sage.

Selingo, J. J. (2013). *College (un)bound: The future of higher education and what it means for students.* New York, NY: Houghton Mifflin Harcourt.

Sternberg, R. (2012, April 3). Failure to change. *Inside Higher Ed.* Retrieved from http://www.insidehighered.com/views/2012/04/03/essay-why-some-colleges-cant-change

CHAPTER 12

Mobilizing Student Affairs for Innovation

Laurence N. Smith and Albert B. Blixt

How can these ideas for making student affairs a hub for campus innovation be applied in real life? This chapter tells how one vice president for student affairs launched an innovation hub to respond to the challenges facing her institution. The case is somewhat fictional, as it combines persons and events from a number of clients with whom we have worked. The situations, events, and outcomes, however, are real.

NORTH STAR UNIVERSITY

North Star University (NSU) is a typical Midwestern public university. It has a total enrollment of 14,000 and offers undergraduate and graduate programs in its colleges of literature, science and the arts, health and human services, business, education, and technology. Founded in 1868, NSU was originally North Star Teacher's College and continues to be well known for its primary and secondary teaching programs. The school is located in Center City, a quiet town of 55,000. NSU is proud of its long history and tradition of preparing students based on the "North Star Way," a set of values established by its first president, the early feminist Cora D. Perkins. These values include excellence, courage, honor, and service to others. The college was private until 1961, when it became part of the state system. It became a university in 1972 with the addition of the College of Health and Human Services. Other colleges followed over the next several years. NSU actively encourages diversity in its hiring and admissions practices.

The school has a 6-year graduation rate just under 34%, well below the average among its peers. Its students come from 24 states, although most come from within the state and the Midwestern region. The significant international student population is drawn primarily from India and China, where NSU has an active recruiting presence.

Freshman enrollment this fall had a 250-student shortfall.

Unfortunately, freshman enrollment this fall had a 250-student shortfall. This fact, combined with a lower number of students returning as sophomores, has resulted in the need to reduce budgets throughout the university.

NORTH STAR UNIVERSITY LEADERSHIP

The university president, Steven Gladwell, was hired 2 years ago when the previous president retired after 19 years. Gladwell commissioned a strategic planning process last year that called for a greater focus on innovation to improve new student enrollment and retention rates. However, this process is still in the beginning stage, owing to institutional inability to compromise and the president's directive to cut back on specific programs and services or find alternative delivery approaches that will save money. "I don't believe in across-the-board reductions because vital services will be adversely affected," Gladwell said.

Gladwell and the provost, Ivana Passmore, have taken the position that before they make a final decision on budget cuts, each segment of the university community must make its own recommendations. They want the community to grapple with the difficulties involved in coming up with a good decision and privately hope that this will help generate a shift in culture that will stimulate innovation as part of the change process.

Julia Goodhart, vice president for student affairs, came to her position recently after having been associate vice president for student affairs at Northeast Central State University, one of NSU's sister schools. Goodhart is known for her overall ability, her willingness to lead, and her penchant for coming up with creative approaches to help students. This is her first experience as a vice president and as a member of the president's cabinet. While she has been well received by her staff, she has not yet established herself among her cabinet peers. Goodhart has been cautious about making significant changes in the student affairs division until she becomes familiar with the NSU culture and decides how she will approach her new role. However, she has become acutely aware of the major fiscal issues facing the university and the division. She is also aware that her division is very vulnerable, as others in the university community have already proposed massive reductions in student affairs to reduce the financial impact on their own areas.

Enrollment and retention problems are two obvious signs of trouble. Less obvious is a lack of reliable data for decision making about enrollment issues and how students feel about their campus experience. A recent student attitude survey conducted by the division revealed that while some students are very happy with NSU, a significant number are not. Goodhart discovered soon after becoming vice president that morale is low across her division for reasons deeply rooted in its past. Her staff members have been so negatively conditioned by their experiences under the previous administration that they are unwilling to generate new ideas or take any risks. The institutional culture continues to support this behavior, even though the president and provost encourage open exploration of new ideas and have indicated that a reluctance to take risks can lead to failure. Goodhart understands that the reluctance of the president and the provost to make the budget cuts themselves reflects their desire to change the deeply ingrained institutional culture of top-down administration, in which people either gave their support or were criticized for not being team players. She realizes that the silo mentality, the exhausting rounds of meetings to make even a small decision, and the unwillingness of individuals to speak out or take initiative have been ways of protecting themselves and their departments and insulating them from change.

Goodhart was impressed by the amount of information the school collected about its students, but disappointed when she tried to access it. When she asked for data about student enrollment trends and retention to graduation rates, Information Technology Director Ted Smiley said, "It's all on the university intranet" and handed her a manual for constructing query protocols and extracting important data. What she found were mountains of raw data but no decision-making analysis. At first she interpreted this as incompetence, but she soon learned that Smiley was simply reluctant to be the source of bad tidings. What he did or didn't tell the president was not public, and no reports were published or on file.

Goodhart was impressed by the amount of information the school collected about its students, but disappointed when she tried to access it.

At the same time, Goodhart's staff members complained that they were overworked and lacked the resources to serve students properly. She discovered that there was no strategic direction or staff training and development program. Some of her best and brightest senior staff were rumored to be considering leaving but were waiting hopefully to see whether she succeeded. It was clear that something had to be done and that she would have to step up to meet that challenge.

The Decision to Act

Goodhart had once heard someone say, "If it is to be, it's up to me." She knew that while many things were out of her control, many others were within her power as vice president. She was an avid reader on leadership topics, especially the sources and wise use of power. In her new role, Goodhart determined that her best course was to make the student affairs division a hub of innovation on the

> *Goodhart had once heard someone say, "If it is to be, it's up to me."*

NSU campus. She set about forging a plan to mobilize her division to create and implement new ideas that would help NSU deal with what could only be called threats to its continued viability. The plan would involve building awareness and understanding about the process of innovation and change, and conveying a sense of urgency to get her division involved in putting new ideas into action.

Before moving ahead, Goodhart met privately with President Gladwell. She described her concerns and her intention to act boldly. The president told her that was why she was hired and asked only that he be kept informed. He noted that the provost, Chief Information Officer Bradley Brightway, and Vice President for Business Administration Joyce Tinsley could be important allies and needed to be informed about what would be taking place and cultivated to ensure their understanding and support. "You need to have allies on the cabinet," Gladwell said. Goodhart said that she had already taken Passmore and Brightway to lunch and they had pledged their support, and she was scheduled to meet with Tinsley later that week. The president replied, "I'm glad to see that you're taking the initiative. You can count on my support as well."

GETTING THE SENIOR LEADERSHIP TEAM ON BOARD

Goodhart's next step was to call a meeting of her newly formed student affairs executive council, which comprised five of her direct reports. She carefully spelled out the facts that made the urgent case for change, including the connection between enrollment shortfalls and the fiscal crisis that was forcing serious budget cuts. The council also reviewed an independent survey administered a few weeks earlier that reported that almost 40% of students were somewhat or very dissatisfied with at least one important aspect of their NSU experience. Complaints included encounters with rude or poorly trained frontline staff, offices that were closed during lunch, bad advice from academic advisors, and scholarship aid that was frontloaded in the first year to attract students and then not available in subsequent years. There were also complaints about courses not being offered each semester that were prerequisites for other courses, which extended the time required to graduate. Many students said they could not get help in defining a clear path to graduation and had trouble seeing the connection between majors and future careers. Some students said career center staff, academic advisors, and even the faculty were not up to date on changes in the workplace and were giving out information that was no longer accurate.

As they discussed these student complaints, executive council members shared some of their own. The associate vice president said that, in the past, negative feedback was unacceptable and anyone who provided it was seen as hostile and not considered to be a team player. Politeness trumped honesty, and candor was seen as rocking the boat. Another council member asked whether being open and talking about problems could be defined as an innovation. "Not in a healthy organization," Goodhart replied.

Council members began describing other ways NSU was falling short. They bemoaned the clumsy and outdated website, the lack of student participation in campus organizations, and the lack of weekend activities, which caused many local students to go home for the weekend. One participant said, "Our students call this 'Suitcase U,' because the place empties out on Friday night." It was noted that students who did remain on campus often complained about the lack of food service and the lack of off-campus transportation for those without cars.

> *Politeness trumped honesty, and candor was seen as rocking the boat.*

One group of students who received insufficient attention was military personnel stationed at the nearby U.S. Air Force base, who often enrolled for 2 years and then were transferred or left the service. This situation contributed to the retention problem, but a council member noted that these personnel "are eager and bright and bring needed credit hours to the university each term." She added, "Many of them would like to continue at NSU, but our online courses are not the ones they need."

The executive council spent the afternoon discussing the problems, listening to Goodhart's plans, and asking questions about what it would take to establish an innovation hub in student affairs. Goodhart laid out her roadmap for an innovation initiative, and everyone agreed. At the end of the meeting, despite the enormity of the challenges, the executive council members reported a new sense of hope, openness, energy, and purpose.

BASIC TRAINING IN INNOVATION AND CHANGE

Two weeks later Goodhart convened a planning and training session for all management-level members of the division. The purpose was to broaden the foundation for leading the innovation and change initiative and to make sure that division leadership at all levels had a full understanding of the goals and objectives.

Following a carefully prepared agenda, Goodhart took the group through the case for change at NSU. She explained the concepts of sustaining and disruptive innovation. The group reviewed five key areas of opportunity for innovation:

1. Responding to changing student demographics;

2. Educating students about the changing world of work and how to prepare for it;

3. Creating efficiencies through the impact of technology;

4. Improving retention and graduation rates; and

5. Responding to student requests for programs and experiences that would inspire them and help them develop meaning and purpose in their lives.

There was a mixture of excitement and anxiety in the group. One person said, "Yes, this is all very important, but what can we do? We're stretched so thin already, and more budget cuts are coming." Goodhart acknowledged their concerns and told them they needed to broaden their thinking. She focused on the leadership dimensions of their roles and emphasized that tough times created not only problems but opportunities as well. She said that if the university could reverse its enrollment difficulties, the financial constraints would be unnecessary. She noted that the student affairs division had a mission to create a positive student experience and that it was obligated to reconsider what part it played in the enrollment crisis and how it could help to improve conditions. She urged the group to stop thinking like managers with limited resources and start thinking like leaders.

Stop thinking like managers with limited resources and start thinking like leaders.

The managers took a brief leadership self-assessment and discussed the results. They began to see that new things could be accomplished with existing resources but that doing so required total divisional understanding and support, as well as ongoing assurances that support would continue if things didn't work out and problems occurred. At the end of the session, Goodhart laid out her plan for involving the entire division in establishing a Student Affairs Innovation Hub.

During the next few weeks the management group held several intensive sessions to identify innovation initiatives in each of the five areas and to decide who would be the best people to serve on the innovation action team for each area. Goodhart noted that decisions about the priority order of innovation efforts and change initiatives would be based on the plans proposed by the innovation action teams.

At the conclusion of the meeting, an evaluation was conducted that allowed anonymous feedback. The results were overwhelmingly positive in their support but also indicated strong concern that the effort would not be sustained when the staff realized its full impact and the changes they would have to make in their daily routines. The feedback made it clear that people were skeptical because of their previous experience. But even with these concerns, there was a strong endorsement for moving forward.

THE INNOVATION RETREAT

One month later the entire division met in the university's conference center for a 2-day retreat to launch the Student Affairs Innovation Hub and the division's new agenda. The dress was casual and the atmosphere relaxed. The purpose statement for the meeting was: "To begin building ourselves as an innovation engine in order to facilitate change at North Star University that will increase the positive impact we have on attracting and retaining our students." The division's executive council strongly recommended that several key university administrators be invited to participate, including vice presidents, deans, and several directors. They were selected on the basis of how the five areas of opportunity would affect their operations.

The participants began by defining four outcomes they wanted from the session:

1. A clear vision of where we are headed.
2. New ideas about things we can do that are a stretch but realistic.
3. A tangible plan for how to bring this back to others on campus.
4. Excitement, motivation, commitment, and unity as a division.

The group did a call-out of the benefits of innovation. They included: "increased influence in the university, being able to chart our own course, realizing the potential of the North Star Way, increasing student engagement, and increased empowerment." They also called out their worries about launching an innovation initiative; these included: "lack of resources, fear of failure, job security, needing to let go of some things we like, being punished for taking risks, and resistance from others." Members of the group seemed relieved to be able to get these pros and cons of innovation out in the open and to discover how much these feelings were shared within the group.

Goodhart reviewed the four-step process of innovation: (1) identify high-value opportunities; (2) generate lots of ideas; (3) test fast, fail fast; and (4) go with what works. The group broke into five work teams, each looking for high-value opportunities in one of the key innovation areas. Each innovation action team was asked to generate both opportunities and a description of what success would look like. When the five teams got together again, each had something exciting to report. Following are some examples.

Team #1 (Changing Demographics) proposed that panels be created to study the similarities and differences among student generations and various student population segments. They suggested that the study focus on students who are digital natives as well as the specific needs of student clusters such as freshmen living on campus, freshmen commuters, transfer students, multicultural students, LGBT (lesbian, gay, bisexual, and transgender) students, and international students. The team also identified solutions to make access to services easier. They envisioned creating a "one-stop shop" for basic services by relocating academic advising, financial aid, and career services to a central location near the student union. At the time, students had to walk across campus to get from one office to another, and some offices were hidden away in obscure parts of the campus. The team wanted to see much better signage and directional kiosks on campus and recommended creating a Welcome Center for prospective students and their families. They also recommended the establishment of a divisional training program for new employees, especially frontline, customer-facing employees, including student workers. They agreed that participation should be required and training should be part of paid work time.

Team #2 (World of Work) suggested expanding the Career Center with programs that combine experiential learning, early career exploration, and special tracks for various populations such as international students, veterans, returning adult learners, and students who intend to pursue graduate studies. The team recommended programs that would encourage first-year students to get out of the classroom and gain some real-world experience. They suggested inviting representatives from various employment sectors to participate in ongoing workshops and seminars on how the world of work was changing, what new jobs were being created, and how to prepare for entrance and success in them. The team also recommended involving alumni in the programs to open doors to employment opportunities.

Team #3 (Technology) focused on how to streamline access to information for students. This team suggested creating an application (app) that could be used on computers, tablets, and other mobile devices that would give students access to calendars, office hours, online services, campus social networking, and suggestions for participating in student interest groups or activities. The team members saw the app as a "personal concierge," perhaps with an interactive voice response system to answer student questions. The team recommended soliciting student input into both the design and maintenance of the app, and allowing monitored open source contributions.

Team #4 (Retention and Graduation) proposed a focused, data-driven effort to increase retention and graduation in specific at-risk target groups, including freshman who are the first in their families to attend college, transfer students, international students, and students in the lowest academic segment of the entering freshman class. The team wanted much better information about who was dropping out or transferring and why. They saw a need to make retention a campuswide effort in which faculty, staff, and administrators all had a role. They noted that simply identifying students at risk is not sufficient; the school needs to have mechanisms for intervening early with these students to see that they get the support they need, whether financial, academic, or mental health related. The team was also clear that students need to take more responsibility for their own

Simply identifying students at risk is not sufficient; the school needs to have mechanisms for intervening early with these students.

success and be empowered to do so. They suggested identifying technologies other schools have used to more effectively support and retain students.

Team #5 (Living the North Star Way) worked on initiatives to help students find meaning and purpose in their lives as part of the student experience. They liked the theme of "preparing to live extraordinary lives," because many students don't see themselves as capable of being extraordinary. The team suggested required service–learning as one avenue for students to make a difference in the world while gaining valuable leadership experience. It also recommended more robust mentoring from faculty, staff, and community members, and matching juniors and seniors with entering freshmen. Finally, the team suggested creating an online game called Life Challenge, in which students meet a series of challenges to gain insight into what matters to them while building analytical skills and earning badges.

After all the teams had reported, Goodhart and the group turned to deciding what an innovation hub might look like. The consensus was that the hub should be a blend of professional staff and online resources that would provide a forum for learning the skills needed for innovation and change. Goodhart said she wanted the hub to function as the research and development laboratory of student affairs and as a model for the rest of the campus. She chose one of her direct reports as the full-time director of the Student Affairs Innovation Hub. Team leaders would be appointed for each of the five innovation areas, with time and responsibilities built into their performance expectations. Team leaders would work with the director of the hub to form innovation action teams and to implement ideas from the retreat, and other ideas as they arose. The team leaders would comprise a steering committee to ensure that the efforts of all the action teams were coordinated. Time lines were established and plans developed for engaging the entire division.

INNOVATION TEAMS

Goodhart was pleasantly surprised at the amount of energy generated by the retreat. Suddenly people were able to see new possibilities. Each of the five innovation action teams included members from across the division and from other areas in the university. In the weeks following the retreat, the teams met to sharpen their concepts and plan how to implement them. Help came from some unexpected sources. The dean of the College of Technology heard about what was going on and arranged for both professors and students in computer science to advise on developing the student affairs app. The president of the North Star Alumni Association offered, with support from the College of Business, to host a campus think tank on preparing for emerging careers. Each team managed to find people on campus who were willing to contribute their expertise. In the end, the five teams developed 11 innovation initiatives that could be accomplished in the first academic year.

In the days following the innovation retreat, the entire staff of the student affairs division learned about the initiatives that were under way, the need for new solutions, and expectations for their involvement. By now painful budget cuts had been put in place, including pay and hiring freezes. There were

Suddenly people were able to see new possibilities.

some layoffs, including 5 persons from the 90-member student affairs staff. Morale would have been lower were it not for a promise from the president that if enrollment could be raised through better recruiting and more effective retention measures, those cuts could be reversed in the following year. Everyone was motivated to do something to attract and keep more students.

While the innovation action teams pursued their goals, Goodhart maintained regular communication with her colleagues on the president's cabinet. Throughout the next 3 months she reported to the cabinet about progress and found herself in several informational conversations with deans and senior administrators. Most of the campus was still unaware of these efforts, but that would soon change.

LAUNCHING CHANGE: THE ALL-CAMPUS MEETING

As interest in the Student Affairs Innovation Hub initiative began to grow throughout the campus, Goodhart believed it was time to hold an innovation workshop to which all students, faculty, and staff were invited. On the day of the workshop, nearly 200 people came to the student union ballroom, which was decorated with signs and posters about innovation. They sat at round tables of eight, with seating carefully designed so that each table was a representative sample of the campus community. President Gladwell opened the meeting with a strong endorsement of the student affairs division's approach to finding new ways to attract, educate, retain, and graduate the next generation of proud NSU students.

> *On the day of the workshop, nearly 200 people came to the student union ballroom, which was decorated with signs and posters about innovation.*

Noting the need to attract "more and better" students, Gladwell pledged his support for making innovation one of the core elements of the North Star Way in the future.

Workshop participants heard about the events, trends, and developments that made innovation and change essential for NSU. They heard about the work being done by student affairs through its Innovation Hub and innovation action teams. They also heard about the new services that were being launched, including the student services app, an early alert and intervention program for at-risk students, a Welcome Center, streamlined student advising, and expanded student leadership development training for leaders of the 147 on-campus student organizations. Participants discussed what they had heard, asked questions, and offered their own suggestions for how best to get these innovations adopted across the campus.

> *Everyone came away with a new sense of community after speaking with people they rarely, if ever, saw and learning that they all shared common goals.*

Everyone came away with a new sense of community after speaking with people they rarely, if ever, saw and learning that they all shared common goals. Enthusiasm for the changes was high.

BUILDING MOMENTUM AND EMBEDDING INNOVATION INTO THE CAMPUS CULTURE

Goodhart and the entire student affairs team knew how quickly good intentions can dissipate if the changes being instituted are not constantly reinforced. A full-scale internal marketing communication campaign reached out to various segments of the student body, including full-time, part-time, online, commuter, and international students. Educational tables were set up in the residence halls and the student union and at each of the colleges, offering students technical assistance in downloading the apps. Everyone in student affairs wore a button that said "Ask Me About Innovation!" and everyone was trained to explain to students, faculty, and staff the benefits of the Innovation Hub. Goodhart and Passmore worked together to form a faculty innovation advisory group to explore how innovation might be brought into the classroom. All of the deans received retention reports on their majors at the beginning of each semester. Within a year, faculty participation in the early alert system had reached 90%.

It soon became impossible to walk across campus or go on social media sites or the NSU website without hearing or seeing something about North Star innovation. Success stories were regularly reported as various initiatives began to show results. Goodhart and her senior staff reviewed progress in experiments and pilot programs. Those that showed promise were continued; those that didn't were phased out quickly. The student affairs division began to live up to its goal of being a learning organization.

> *Results began to be seen across the entire campus.*

Results began to be seen across the entire campus. Over the following year, first-to-second-year student retention rose by 7%. New strategies increased the enrollment yield enough to slightly exceed projections for the entering fall class. The Honors College found that it needed new classrooms and residence hall space, as its numbers nearly doubled with the enrollment of more highly qualified students. With the numbers in hand for the next fall enrollment, President Gladwell unlocked the hiring freeze and began to fund restoration of some positions. However, he did so with a new focus on funding programs that offered the most return on the money spent. Often these were ideas that came from the Innovation Hub.

One indicator of the success of the Innovation Hub concept was that North Star University was able to sponsor a regional innovation symposium that was attended by many colleges and universities from the five-state area. Julia Goodhart was the keynote speaker.

WRITE YOUR OWN STORY

Goodhart's story has a happy ending. You have an opportunity to write your own innovation story. First you must make the decision to act. Then you will need to grow as a leader as you enter the uncharted territory of shaping the future. You will need some courage and a willingness to embrace uncertainty. The ideas and tools in this book can be your guide. It is our hope that you will set out on that journey and that you will find success.

CHAPTER 13

The Way Forward

Laurence N. Smith and Albert B. Blixt

If you have come this far in the book, it is obvious that you are serious about creating a positive and sustainable future. The ideas presented here are not a recipe for using innovation and change to get to that future. You cannot copy and paste them into your leadership role. Instead, they are tools that you will need to experiment with and make your own. You will need to integrate these concepts with your own expertise and experience. They do provide perspective and a set of choices for how you will respond to what confronts you.

NAVIGATING CHANGE

Dealing with innovation and change brings two images to mind. The first is the image of whitewater rafting on the Colorado River.

It is essential to have the right equipment, the right team, and the right preparation before setting out. The pilot needs to know as much as possible about the twists and turns that the raft is likely to encounter. The team needs to be well trained and agree on how its members will work together to get through the rapids. Still, once on the river, the pilot and the team will need to react to conditions that could not be predicted. They will need to be alert to what is happening and adjust what they are doing to avoid the rocks. No matter how many times they have navigated the river, old hands will tell you that it is never the same twice.

But with preparation, focus, and teamwork, the raft can emerge into the calm waters below and prepare for the next set of rapids. One of the great skills in whitewater rafting is to keep control while going with the flow of the river. Attempts to stay safe in the shallows can lead to disaster. In leading innovation and change in higher education, the chief student affairs officer (CSAO) needs to prepare to respond to the unexpected and to make sure everyone on the team is pulling together. The leader must also embrace the danger of taking risks. Recognizing the difficulty of bringing about change, many executives may try to avoid the risk of failure by not trying.

One of the great skills in whitewater rafting is to keep control while going with the flow of the river.

Whether this comes from a reluctance to confront the culture in which they work, their conditioning from past experiences, obeying common wisdom, not wanting to rock the boat, fear of rejection, or some other reason, they see a closed, locked door to opportunity. They do not act. But because they do not act, the risk becomes even greater. The lesson is that you are already on the river. You have no choice.

The second image comes from the last stanza of Robert Frost's (1916) poem "The Road Not Taken":

> I shall be telling this with a sigh
> Somewhere ages and ages hence:
> Two roads diverged in a wood, and I—
> I took the one less traveled by,
> And that has made all the difference. (p. 9)

Is taking the road less traveled a wise or reckless decision? Is the sigh one of relief or disappointment? Whether or not a CSAO is inspired to assume a leadership role to create a thriving, dynamic future for the division of students affairs will determine how these words will be interpreted. Traveling the road less taken does not have to be a lonely journey and certainly not one of disappointment. As Peter Skarzynski and Rowan Gibson (2008) pointed out, "One of the great myths of innovation . . . is that breakthrough ideas are produced solely by intuitive individuals or by small creative teams working in isolation" (p. 36). Usually innovation comes from interacting and networking with a rich and diverse community of people; not as the product of individual brilliance or an effort of a few individuals.

The trip down the less traveled road provides the CSAO with the opportunity to stretch the boundaries of the division of student affairs for his or her personal development as a leader of innovation and change, and to stretch the role of the division of student affairs as a vital force in determining the future of the college or university. There will be many companions to travel with. They can come from both within and outside the institution. As knowledge about the journey becomes more widespread, others will want to join the travelers on the road. Who knows? Given the power of social marketing and its potential for creating large group action, the number of travelers on the road might become a parade.

Skarzynski and Gibson (2008) posed the following question to determine campus efficacy: "Has your [college or university] reached the stage at which many or all of your colleagues believe that innovation is part of their job?" (p. 45). As CSAO, it is important that you do not close the door to newcomers but invite others who have the ability to be leaders, innovators, and change agents or who control the resources for financing the journey to join the parade of travelers.

Keep in mind this evaluation by management expert Joe Batten (1989):

> Tomorrow's leaders [need to] be, above all, mentally tooled for the decades ahead. Pushed and driven organizations will certainly lose out to those that are led and stretched. We must release old habits and consign them to the past. The cold, hard, rigid driver is out. The leading, stretching, expective [sic], intuitive leader plugged into productive, future-oriented attitudes . . . is in. The orderly, antiseptic climate is out. The yeasty, fermentive [sic], and volatile climate is in. (p. 5)

Successful innovators must have the courage to fail and the strength to keep on innovating. Failure is a great teacher of what doesn't work. The lesson learned is not to try harder but to try a different approach to innovate and change.

The leading, stretching, expective, intuitive leader plugged into productive, future-oriented attitudes . . . is in.

PITFALLS TO AVOID

Innovation is hard work. Charles Prather and Lisa Gundry (1995) provided advice on avoiding some common missteps. It is important as a leader to avoid the five pitfalls that hinder innovation: (1) identifying the wrong problem, (2) judging ideas too quickly, (3) stopping with the first good idea, (4) failing to get the right people on board, and (5) obeying rules that don't exist.

Identifying the wrong problem. Just because there is widely held agreement as to the root cause of problems and what needs to be changed, doesn't mean that it is correct. It is imperative that the CSAO ensures that due diligence is exercised and analysis is undertaken to determine cause and effect. Remember that leaders do the right things; managers do things right. The CSAO's leadership efforts should focus on doing the right things, so that when they are done right they make the intended difference.

Judging ideas too quickly. Although judging requires divergent thinking, there is a tendency for "people to judge ideas too quickly, thereby effectively squelching the creative process. All employees (but especially the experts) need to understand the distinction between divergent and convergent thinking, and need to learn to put their tendency to converge 'on hold' at certain times, to allow new ideas to flourish" (Prather & Gundry, 1995, pp. 19–20).

Stopping with the first good idea. As Prather and Gundry (1995) noted, "The first idea is never best because . . . it is the easiest to come up with [and] is generally derived from brainstorming [which] isn't set up to change thinking" (p. 20). The best ideas (those most likely to be implemented) "occur after the ability to generate ideas via brainstorming has been exhausted" (p. 20).

> *Remember that leaders do the right things; managers do things right.*

Failing to get the right people on board. There are people who support you and there are others who can derail the innovation and change initiative. Special effort needs to be made to include potential disruptors early in the process and convert them into supporters.

Obeying rules that don't exist. Policies and rules that don't exist, but are thought to, deter leaders from pursuing action. Also, there are policies and rules that do exist that frustrate initiative and often deter it. It is critical to check whether or not the policies and rules really do exist, and if they do, to seek an exception. In some institutions the predominant culture thinks that it is easier to act without seeking permission and to ask for forgiveness later.

A THRIVING FUTURE

Gary Hamel (2000) shared useful insights in his book *Leading the Revolution*. He noted that "the gap between what can be imagined and what can be accomplished has never been smaller. . . . [F]or the first time in history we can work backward from our imagination rather than forward from our past" (p. 10). Hamel observed that the age of progress (rigorous planning, continuous improvement, statistical process control, six sigma, reengineering, and enterprise resource planning) has given way to the age of revolution due to dramatic advances in the multiple areas of technology that touch just about every aspect of our lives. He wrote:

> We have developed the capacity to interrupt history. . . . Our heritage is no longer our destiny. . . Each of us must become a dreamer, as well as a doer. Our collective selves—our organizations—must also learn to dream. In many organizations there has been a massive failure of collective imagination. How else can one account for the fact that so many organizations have been caught flat-footed by the future? (Hamel, 2000, pp. 10–11)

Hamel's (2000) point is that "the goal is not to speculate on what might happen, but to imagine what you can actually make happen" (p. 119). To this we add, *"And to make it happen!"* It is our dreams that will provide the framework for harnessing and focusing our energy to create innovations and to implement them. For example, who would have thought that two young men named Steve Jobs

> *It is our dreams that will provide the framework for harnessing and focusing our energy to create innovations and to implement them.*

and Bill Gates with just passion and a dream would create two companies that would transform our world? Everyone can dream and by doing so help to define the future in which they will survive and thrive.

The journey of creating transformational change is long and complex, but rewarding. It is our hope that CSAOs will take the road less traveled to help create something new as highly involved, assertive leaders of innovation and change. Doing so will ensure a thriving future for institutions of higher education and student affairs.

REFERENCES

Batten, J. (1989). *Tough-minded leadership.* New York, NY: AMACON/ American Management Association.

Frost, R. (1916). *Mountain interval.* New York, NY: Henry Holt.

Hamel, G. (2000). *Leading the revolution.* Boston, MA: Harvard Business School Press.

Prather, C. W., & Gundry, L. K. (1995). *Blueprints for innovation: How creative processes can make you and your company more competitive.* New York, NY: American Management Association.

Skarzynski, P., & Gibson, R. (2008). *Innovation to the core: A blueprint for transforming the way your company innovates.* Boston, MA: Harvard Business Review Press.

Afterword

Creating innovative and transformational change is an ongoing process. As we send this book to press, we are developing companion publications. We invite readers to contact us to ask questions, offer ideas, and share stories. Send us an e-mail and let us know how change initiatives are progressing at your institution.

Laurence N. Smith

smith@newcampusdynamics.com

Albert B. Blixt

alblixt@newcampusdynamics.com

Index